A Slave Set
Free

A Slave Set Free

John Newton

Irene Howat

CF4·K

© Copyright 2003 Irene Howat
Reprinted 2004 and 2008
ISBN 978-1-85792-834-1

Published by
Christian Focus Publications
Geanies House, Fearn, Tain, Ross-shire,
IV20 1TW, Scotland, U.K.

www.christianfocus.com
email: info@christianfocus.com

Cover design Alister Macinnes
Cover Illustration Pete Roberts

Printed and bound in Denmark
by Nørhaven Paperback A/S

For Grace

Contents

Who is a Slave?

James kicked his football as hard as he possibly could. It went over the fence, across the lane and into the wood on the other side.

'What did you do that for?' his friend, Chris, called from the next-door bedroom window.

James swung round and grinned. 'How long have you been watching me?'

But he spoke to an empty window. Chris was on his way downstairs. He would answer the question face to face.

'So how long were you spying?' James demanded. 'Did you see me doing 34 headers against the wall without dropping the ball?'

Chris admitted that he had. 'But I can do better than that!' he added.

'Let's see you,' James challenged.

His friend shrugged. 'I would if there was a ball. And you've still not told me why you kicked it into the wood.'

James wasn't about to tell Chris that he'd kicked the ball into the wood because he was cross for being sent out for some fresh air and exercise. James had wanted to stay in and play with the computer. Smirking at

Chris, James yelled, 'Race you to the ball!' and sprinted off in the direction of the garden gate.

The pair of them ran across the lane and ducked under a branch that had broken the fence at the side of the wood. It was where they always went through. And it led to where they'd had a den until they were too big for it.

'Did you see where the ball landed?' James asked. 'I didn't notice.'

Chris looked around. 'Over beside the stumps, I think.'

They walked deeper into the wood.

'I've won!' James yelled, grabbing the ball from behind a clump of long grass before his friend saw it.

Sitting down on the tree stumps, the two boys discussed Saturday's football match. The local team was playing at home against a team at the top of the league.

'They haven't a chance of winning,' Chris decided, 'not unless they take you through the tunnel with them. That was some kick I saw from the window.'

James knew his friend was fishing for what was bothering him.

'It's not fair,' he said. 'I wasn't disturbing anyone and nobody else wanted to use the computer. But Dad had made his mind up. I got the usual story, "When I was your age I was out kicking a ball around until bedtime. Your generation is going to grow up without ever having been young. You're just a slave to that computer."'

Chris grinned.

'I've had the same lecture,' Chris admitted, 'but it usually blows over by the time I come and play some of your computer games!'

Grabbing the ball from his friend, Chris headed it against a chestnut tree.

'You'll never get 34 there,' teased James. 'The tree's too rough.'

And it was. After only eight headers, the ball hit a branch and fell too far to the side for Chris to head it back again.

'Want to go back and be a slave to your computer again?' the boy asked.

Shaking his head, James said he thought it was still a bit too soon for his dad to have changed his mind.

The two boys sat down on the stumps again.

'I wonder what it would be like to be a slave to a computer,' commented Chris. 'You'd have to delete everything because one key says delete. And you'd have to insert things every time you looked at the insert key.'

James laughed. 'Everything you wrote would be in capitals because you'd have to obey the key that says Caps Lock.'

Chris pointed out that they'd have to leave the computer every time they noticed the key that said Shift!

'I think Dad must have been looking at the keyboard and saw the Escape key and that's why he told me to take a break from it!'

'Which all goes to prove that you're not a slave to the computer because slaves couldn't escape!'

'Try telling Dad that,' grumped James.

'I wonder what it was like for real slaves,' Chris said, after a couple of minutes.

James looked at him. 'You shouldn't have spoken then,' he said. 'I was thinking about the Pause key.'

'Yes, I should,' Chris announced. 'And whether you like it or not we're going to talk about what it was like for real slaves until we can get back to the computer.'

'Why should I?' James grunted.

'Because I'm using the Control key!' Chris laughed.

That knocked James out of his bad mood and he smiled

'OK,' he agreed. 'You win. Slaves it is.'

Chris, who had always been a good storyteller, looked around where they were sitting.

'Imagine this is a forest in Africa,' he began. 'And we're the village lookouts. Rumours are spreading that strange creatures have been seen in the deepest and darkest parts of the forest.'

'What kind of strange creatures?' James asked.

'Very strange. There were four of them, two lots of two. And they looked like white monkeys, only they weren't hairy.'

'Where were they last seen?' James asked, looking around him at the trees.

'Down by the river,' Chris replied, really getting into his story. 'But I've not told you the worst yet.'

'What's that?'

'These creatures are cleverer than monkeys because they have made a fire and are cooking on it. Now imagine that we've suddenly been jumped on. We realise that these creatures are not monkeys but two white men!'

'Even more scary!' James pretended to shiver. 'Especially if you'd never seen a white man before!'

Chris stood up for the next part of the story. 'Now they tie your right hand to my left hand and your right ankle to my left ankle. Then they tie one end of a rope round my neck and the other end round your neck.'

'Why do they do that? If they want us for slaves there is no point in strangling us.'

'That is the point! They tie us like that so we can't run away. And they lead us back to where they have other captured villagers.'

'Is anyone we know there?' asked James.

Chris pretended to look around. 'No,' he said. 'No one. And nobody speaks our language. We've got no idea what is going to happen to us or where we are being taken. We will never see anyone we know ever again. By the way, the only food we will get are plant roots, leaves and nuts.' Chris was getting really carried away. 'Then we are tied to total strangers and led for miles and miles through the forest until we come to the coast. Then we are dumped in the hold of a ship and we never see Africa ever again. And when the ship goes out to sea we are terrified because we have never seen the sea before and we think that we will drop off the edge of it!'

James had just picked up the ball when both boys stopped dead. There was the sound of cracking twigs close by, though they couldn't see what had made the noise.

A voice called, 'James! Chris! Can you hear me?'

'It's Dad!' James sighed, relieved that it wasn't a fearsome slave trader or worse.

'I thought I might find you here,' he said. 'I'm glad you've discovered your den again.'

The boys looked at each other, each thinking the same thing. It was years since they'd played in their den. After all, they weren't kids anymore!

'When I suggested you went out to play,' said Mr Dawson, 'I didn't expect you still to be away at dinner time.'

James suddenly realised that his stomach was rumbling.

'I hope we get more than plant roots, leaves and nuts for dinner,' Chris commented.

Mr Dawson looked at Chris, 'Have your parents become vegetarians or something?'

Chris and James laughed so much they could hardly breathe.

'Will you come in later?' James asked, as he and Chris parted company at the garden gate.

Chris looked at Mr Dawson.

'OK,' the man smiled. 'You've had some fresh air and exercise. You can play on the computer tonight.'

'Play!' said James, trying to sound both surprised and indignant. 'We don't want to play. We've got some research to do.'

He winked at his friend.

'Historical research,' Chris agreed. 'Eighteenth century, I think.'

Mr Dawson decided he'd missed out on something and dropped the subject.

'That'll be Chris,' Dad said, when the doorbell rang less than an hour later.

James let his friend in.

'Is it all right if we use the computer?' he asked his father.

'Yes,' Mr Dawson said. 'Provided you don't waste too long on games.'

'We're not going to be playing games,' Chris reminded him. 'We want to do some research about slavery.'

'Is this homework?' Dad asked.

'No,' his son said. 'Just something we're interested in.'

'What inspired that sudden interest?' queried Mr Dawson.

James smiled at his father. 'You did,' he told him. 'It was something you said this afternoon.'

Mr Dawson picked up his newspaper.

'Slavery,' he thought. 'I never even mentioned the word!'

In the hour that followed, James and Chris researched the subject of slavery and were both fascinated and appalled by what they read.

'Look,' Chris said, as they prepared to close down the computer. 'There's a bit here about a book for teenagers. It says it's about a slave ship captain. He's called John Newton.'

'I'll ask Dad if we can send for it,' decided James.

'John Newton might be just the man to tell us what slavery was really like.'

Meeting on Little Bear Quay

Four boys, dressed in rags, scrambled over the great coils of rope that stood tall as men in the alley at the side of the ships' chandler's store, an amazing building filled with everything a seaman could possibly need. The game they were playing was so mischievous that they had posted a lookout at the end of the alley on Little Bear Quay. When the lookout whistled, the other boys came running. 'Come and see this!' the lad on the Quay shouted. 'We've got a prop'r littl' gent comin' our way!' His friends knew exactly who was coming. It was John Newton, son of Captain Newton, and they thought it was the best of all fun to laugh at him.

John stared straight ahead as he walked along the Quay, not daring to look to the side in case he caught the eye of any of the young ruffians. And he felt silly. Deep in his heart he would gladly have exchanged his fine clothes for their rags if he had been able to join in their game. How he would have loved to scramble with them over the coils of rope, to dodge the chandler's whip when the man got fed up with their antics, and to run wild around the London docks as they did. He has seen them at Billingsgate being chased by a sailor and he had seen them hoisting themselves up the walls of the great Tower of London. And each time he had looked away, embarrassed for being the young gentleman he was.

Stomping along the road, John thought, 'Why do I have to wear stupid velvet breeches with buckles at the knees. And these woollen stockings are horrid; all they do is make my legs itchy. And I hate the wretched long coat and my yellow waistband looks awful. I look like a little old man instead of a boy. I wish I was like these other boys.' Suddenly John realised that he had been speaking aloud, and that the lads in the alley had heard him. He blushed deeply.

'Why wid a young gent like you wan' to be lik us?' the lookout asked.

John wasn't sure if he should reply.

The same question was asked again.

'I can't run about and play wearing these clothes,' John tried to explain.

Several of the lads giggled at John's proper way of speaking.

'And I don't have friends like you all do,' the boy went on.

'But yer ole man's Cap'n Newt'n,' the lookout said. 'Are ye not friends with the other cap'ns' sons?'

John shook his head. 'No,' he blurted out. 'I don't even know if any of the other captains have sons my age.'

'So who do ye play wi?' one of the lads demanded.

'Play?' John said. 'I don't think I do play. I've never really learned to play.'

The lookout signalled to his gang of friends to go into the alley. The little gentleman made to walk towards the Tower of London when he heard a noise behind him.

'Psst! Psst!' He turned round.

'Ye can join the gang fur the day,' the lookout said. 'But you'll have to hide yer posh clothes behind the ropes. We're not doin' the docks wi' ye lookin' like that,' he announced, pointing at the breeches.

John peeled them off, removed his itch-making socks, rolled his long coat into a bundle with the rest of his clothes and put the bundle, plus his shoes, between the biggest coil of rope and a bin full of iron cleats, the kind that was used for securing chains to ships' timbers. He roughed up his hair in an effort to be more like the others and only succeeded in looking like a well-scrubbed, well brought up lad who had forgotten to put most of his clothes on and brush his hair. He did not look in the least like a street urchin.

That day was an eye-opener to young John Newton. He had been around the docks of London since before he could remember; yet he discovered more in that one day than he'd learned in all of his six-and-a-half years. He wanted to tell his mother all about it, but how could he possibly do that? And he had so much to ask her. By three in the afternoon, John was dressed and more like himself – if unusually dirty – and it was time to go home. His mother was in bed when he arrived, he could hear her cough coming from the bedroom. That gave him time to scrub himself clean before he went in to see her. Having checked himself over, he knocked on his mother's bedroom door.

'Come in,' a weak voice called.

John entered.

'How are you feeling?' he asked, seeing his mother's pale face and the dark rings under her eyes.

Mrs. Newton tried to sit up, but as the effort of moving made her go into a spasm of coughing, she lay back on her pillows.

'I've had a quiet day,' she said softly. 'But I've slept off and on so it has passed quite quickly. What have you done with yourself?'

John, who loved his mother very much, did not want to lie, so he thought for a minute before beginning his story.

'I went down to the Tower of London then walked along to the Little Bear Quay. I met some boys there and stayed with them until it was time to come home.'

'Were they nice boys?' his mother asked, concerned for her son's safety.

'They were nice to me,' he answered truthfully. 'And they knew so much that I didn't know. I learned a lot from them.'

Mrs. Newton was reassured. 'That's good,' she said. 'What sort of things did you learn?'

John knew this was going to be difficult, but

something in him made him need to tell his mother what he had seen.

'There's a ships' chandler there,' he began, 'and there are such interesting things stacked around his shop. There was a great stack of iron collars with small iron rings attached to them. And do you know, Mum,' he went on, 'the collars are put round slaves' necks and they are chained to the ship by the little rings. I didn't know that till the boys told me.'

His mother sighed. She wanted to stop her son going on, but she knew that what he was saying was true and it was better that he talked to her about it than went to bed and had nightmares.

'What else did you see?' she asked. 'Did your new friends show you anything else?'

John, who had been standing beside his mother's bed, kicked off his shoes, and lay down on top of the bed beside her.

'Have you ever seen a mouth-opener?' he asked.

Mrs. Newton said she had not.

'It's a wedge that's used to force slaves to open their mouths. The pointed end is pushed between their teeth then the screw is turned and turned until their mouths are open wide enough to force food down their throats.'

'But why do these poor people not want to eat their food?' she wondered aloud.

John knew the answer. 'It's because they would rather die than go far away from their families to be slaves.'

His mother shuddered. 'I wish you didn't know about neck rings and mouth wedges,' she said, 'but I won't always be here to protect you from things that are ugly.'

John sat bolt upright. 'Where are you going?' he demanded. 'Are you going away somewhere?'

Mrs. Newton shook her head and smiled.

'I'm not fit to go anywhere,' she told him. 'I'm hardly able to get out of bed most days, so I won't be running away to sea.'

John smiled at the thought. And because he was tired, he didn't try to work out what his mother must have meant. Had he done so, he would not have slept as soundly as he did after such an exciting day.

The following morning, Mrs. Newton was feeling a little better. She was able to be up and to do John's lessons with him.

'You are such a clever boy,' she told him, 'I think it is time we started studying Latin together. Do you think you are ready to learn another language?'

John grinned at the thought.

'Yes,' he said, 'I'm sure I am. Will I be able to speak to people in Latin by the time I'm seven?' he asked.

It was his mother's turn to smile.

'I don't think so,' she said. 'You see, Latin is a language you read rather than speak. It's an ancient language, and it helps you understand how we speak today. Also there are ancient books, especially Christian books, that are in Latin and not in English.'

This was so confusing that John changed the subject completely.

'When did I start learning to read English?' he asked.

'I can't remember when you actually began reading,' his mother said, 'but by the time you were four you could read perfectly apart from very long hard words.'

The lad thought about that. 'Well, I think it is time I learned Latin,' he agreed, 'because I've been able to read English on its own for long enough.'

A week or two later Mrs. Newton had a visit from her minister, Rev. David Jennings.

'How is young John?' the minister asked.

'He's a remarkable boy,' the woman said. 'He learns things so quickly, some good and some terrible things.'

Seeing Mr. Jennings puzzled expression, she explained about the Latin and the neck collars and mouth wedges.

'He's young to be learning Latin,' the man said. 'And it's a sad world that makes a six-year-old learn about the slave trade.'

'Sir,' Mrs. Newton said seriously, 'I'm an ill woman and I may not live to see John grow up. It's my heart's desire that he should become a minister. That's why I've started teaching him Latin so early. While I'm alive and able I'll teach him everything I can that will help him get to university.'

Mr. Jennings looked at her serious face. 'Whatever you teach the boy,' he said, 'make sure he knows his Bible.'

Having prayed with Mrs. Newton, the minister rose to go. 'Not only will that good woman not see young John grow up,' he thought, as he walked towards his home, 'it'll be a miracle if she sees his next birthday.'

One morning, just before John was seven, he had a rude awakening.

'Get up!' his father ordered. 'You're mother is not well enough to give you lessons today so you're coming with me.'

John shot out of bed, dressed in double-quick time, and was out the door before he had even said 'Hello' to his mother.

Captain Newton walked on land as he walked when he was at sea, rolling from side to side as though the streets of London were rocking in a force eight gale. Along crowded streets they went as they headed in the direction of the docks.

'Good morning, Captain Newton,' several people said, smiling at the man as they went by.

Somehow that surprised John. It hadn't occurred to him that people would smile and speak to his father on the street.

John glanced up at the man beside him. He was wearing a three cornered hat, a bright coloured waistcoat, a smart coat with silver buttons and he had large silver buckles on his shoes. The boy decided that people were saying 'Good morning' because his father looked good rather than because they liked him. And once, when he looked back at two men who had greeted his father, he saw them smirking and nodding in his direction. When he saw that, he decided he was right.

When Captain Newton stopped to talk to two sailors John listened carefully. His father was speaking a different language! And the three men were speaking so quickly it just seemed to the boy to be a babble of sound.

'Was that Latin you were speaking?' he asked, when they left the men and started walking again.

Captain Newton laughed, not a nice laugh. 'Latin!' he spat. 'That was Spanish! And Spanish is a useful language because people actually speak it. Teaching you Latin is just one of your mother's silly ideas. You're not going to be a minister, boy. You'll be a seaman like your father. And there are a lot of seamen who speak Spanish. You'd be far better learning that than all the things your mother teaches you.'

John opened his mouth to speak but closed it again quickly. His father was going into one of his ugly moods.

World's End and Beyond

John lay in bed unable to sleep. He could hear his father's voice in the next room, and what he heard frightened him. It was especially frightening that his mother's cough was sometimes so harsh and loud that he couldn't hear his father speaking over it.

'You can't stay here in the state you're in,' Captain Newton said. 'There's nobody to look after you and the boy's no help either.'

John shivered. In the silence that followed, he realised his mother was speaking. Kneeling on his bed, with his ear against the wall, he struggled to hear what she was saying.

'My friend, Mrs. Catlett would look after me and maybe nurse me back to health,' he heard her say.

'She'll have a hard job doing that but you'd be better there than here,' Captain Newton barked.

The boy couldn't work out what was happening. He knew his mother often had to stay in bed and that her cough was getting worse and worse, but he could not be sure how serious it was because his father sounded more cross than upset.

But when the day came that his mother was wrapped in rugs and put in a horse-drawn carriage for the journey to Chatham, he did not want to say 'Goodbye' to her. He was scared that he might not see her again.

Shortly afterwards John had a letter from his mother. Taking it to his room, he sat on his bed and read it aloud.

'My dear John, I hope you are well and that you are being a good son. My friend Mrs. Catlett is looking after me very well. My room is kept hot and dark with the windows and all the cracks sealed to keep out the outside air. Even the keyhole is stuffed with a rag! I've often heard it said to someone with consumption, 'When the air comes through a hole take care of your soul.' Well, there's no fresh air reaching me at all. Mrs. Catlett is cooking all the things that are meant to be good for someone in my condition, but I confess I don't like snail broth at all. And the medicines! Ugh! I hope they do me good for they are quite awful to take. My cough is not yet any better but perhaps the medicines will help. I am praying for you, John, that you'll be a good boy and that you'll remember all I've taught you about the Lord. God bless you, with much love, Mum.'

The boy smiled at the rag in the keyhole and the thought of snail broth turned his stomach. But when he read 'remember all I've taught you about the Lord' it seemed to him as though his mother was saying 'Goodbye.' And she was. Before John's seventh birthday his mother had died.

Over the year that followed his mother's death John led a strange sort of life. His father was at sea and he was more or less left to do what he liked. One of the first things to go was his Latin, for his mother had been his teacher and he had only done it to please her. Much of his time was spent around the docks, watching as cargoes were loaded and unloaded. He knew where many of the ships came from and what was in their holds. Some ships carried as much as 40,000 chests of tea, others brought wool, hides, preserved meats and tallow. Even metals like copper arrived by ship at London docks. Then there were the Spanish boats, with holds full of oranges, lead and cork. And ships came from even further away to the East bringing dried fruits, cocoa, spices and many other interesting things as well. The sailors were a constant source of interest. John tried to work out where they came from. There were tall fair men from Scandinavia, short dark men from Brazil and Mexico; there were Cubans and Chileans, and sailors from Manilla and the Philippine Islands. It was one of his games to work out where the men he saw came from.

Although John enjoyed the life he was living, his enjoyment came to an end quite suddenly when his father arrived back from sea. Before he really knew what was happening, he found himself sitting with his father in a hired hackney carriage and heading out of London. The journey was an exciting one for an eight-year-old. They passed the Aldgate market, where carts piled high with hay blocked the way. Then they passed through Wapping and Stepney.

'What's the next place we come to?' the boy asked his father.

'World's End,' Captain Newton grumped.

John thought he had misheard.

'I beg your pardon,' he said.

'The next place we come to is World's End,' repeated his father.

Until they reached the village of World's End, John spent the time wondering if the world really did come to an end so near to London.

Some miles later a strange thing happened. Throughout their journey nobody paid any attention to them at all. But as they went into the village of Aveley people waved at Captain Newton, some even called out to him.

'How do they know my father?' John wondered, glancing sideways at the Captain, who obviously recognised the people. 'And how does he know them?'

It was all very odd and it became odder still. John was taken to a house full of people, none of whom he had ever seen before. One of them, the daughter of the house, was about to become his stepmother. Captain Newton had decided to get married again. Although his stepmother seemed willing enough to care for him, soon after his father remarried, John was sent off to boarding school.

'Newton!' the schoolmaster yelled, 'have you no brains?'

That seemed to be said so often that John wondered if he did have a brain after all.

'Why is it,' he asked himself, 'that I can say my times tables and do my arithmetic when I'm not in the classroom, and then, when the master asks me, it all goes out of my head and I can hardly speak let alone give the answer?'

Sometimes, in bed at night, the boy remembered how his mother had taught him, how they used to read and talk and count and laugh together. Then he had loved to read, now he was almost scared to be seen with a book in case he was asked questions about it and was unable to answer. Having been a happy enough boy back home in London, John Newton became a miserable lad at a boarding school in Stratford, and he was often bottom of the class.

John occasionally thought about the letter his mother had written to him, telling him about her time with the Catletts, and he spent the minutes before falling asleep composing in his mind a letter about the school. Sadly, he had nobody he could send such a letter to. 'Lessons begin at 6 o'clock in the morning,' he began his imaginary letter, 'and we have half an hour for breakfast before lessons begin again. They then go on until 12 noon. In the afternoon we work for another three or four hours. The food is awful and there isn't anything like enough. All the boys are hungry nearly all of the time.' He would have finished his imaginary letter with, 'I want to come home', but he didn't really want to go home at all.

School holidays were short, but in the summer of his ninth year John spent some time at sea. He dreaded going back to Stratford. What he didn't know was that the cruel master had left and a new, kind, one had come in his place.

'How much Latin do you know?' he asked John one day.

'My mother taught me some, but I think I've forgotten it all,' the boy admitted.

The master smiled. 'It'll be inside your head somewhere. Let's see if we can find it and add some more to it. Latin's an interesting language and you'll be able to read about all sorts of ancient battles when you've learned enough to read the books.'

John's second year at school was very different from the first, and he was actually top of the class that year for Latin. Then, although he was just ten years old, the lad left school and he never went back.

There were unwelcome changes in his home around the time John left school, as that was when his new baby stepbrother was born. He was named William. And when Captain Newton came home from sea he hardly noticed his elder son at all, he was so taken up with his wife and William. John tried to get his father's attention but eventually gave up because when he succeeded it was most often to get a row.

* * *

'Are you coming to look for chestnuts?' some boys from the village asked him that autumn.

John agreed to go, and they had a splendid day together.

'What are you going to do when you leave school?' one asked him.

'I've already left school,' John explained. 'And I suppose I'll go to sea like my father.'

'Where does he go?' a red-haired lad asked.

'Mostly to the Mediterranean.'

'What does he take there?' the lad wanted to know.

'It's often English cloth,' John explained. 'The women in Spain and France and Italy like to wear clothes made from it.'

The red-head had his next question ready. 'And what does he bring back with him.'

John grinned. 'He sometimes brings back cloth from the countries he goes to, because that's what English women like their dresses made of.'

The boys laughed. 'You mean he takes cloth from England to make Italian ladies' dresses and he brings cloth from Italy to make English ladies' dresses?'

For the first time John saw the funny side of it.

'I suppose I'll do that too,' he laughed, 'though it does seem crazy.'

That autumn and winter John fell in love with the lovely countryside round about Aveley. He had been brought up in London and to him the country was full of new and interesting things to discover. As well as collecting chestnuts, he gathered beechnuts and blackberries. He watched the geese gathering to fly south for the winter, and he loved to sit on a tree stump under a rookery listening to hundreds of rooks cawing above him. Some evenings he stayed out after dark to see badgers playing, and he liked the evening sound of hedgehogs snuffling. 'How do they make so much noise?' he wondered. 'They sound like baby William when his nose is stuffed up.' And the early morning was another of John's favourite times, especially the following spring, when the birds seemed to be so pleased to see the sunlight that they sang their little hearts out.

'You know almost as much about the country as we do,' one of his friends told him. 'You should stay here in Aveley and work on the land.'

John could think of nothing better than to gather willows for weaving fences, or to learn to be a thatcher, or to work with the cattle and sheep or grow crops. But he knew that could never be. His father was a seaman and he would be a seaman too.

The day to start work came too soon. On John Newton's eleventh birthday he boarded his father's ship and began his working life. He watched as the wind caught the sails high above him, and felt the boat begin to heave away from the dockside. The sound of waves slapping the side of the boat merged with the movement of the sea and they were off. But there was no time to take farewell of England for there was work to be done.

'Can I sleep below with the deck-boys?' John asked his father, at the end of his first day's work.

Captain Newton was horrified. 'My son will share my cabin and eat at my table! You may be doing the work of a deck-boy, but you're the Captain's son and don't you forget it!'

There was no way John could forget who he was. Although the boys would have gladly been friends with him, they couldn't be. The Captain made sure of that. He was fond of his son, but sadly he was quite unable to show it. So, while his first real voyage had its exciting side, it was a lonely experience for young John Newton.

Life on the Ocean Wave

As a small boy John Newton had loved listening to sailors speaking, though he often didn't understand the languages they used. But on board his father's ship the language was English so there was no problem understanding what was being said. Even when words were new to him he could work out what they meant. Although nobody told him, John knew that he was hearing words that he should never use, and that if he ever did and his father found out he would be severely beaten. So he collected these swear words in his head even though he didn't say them, or at least he didn't say them when his father could hear.

And there were other words that bothered the boy when he first heard them. His mother had often talked to him about God the Father and the Lord Jesus Christ. But the sailors, when they said God's name, seemed to spit the words out, where his mother had always said them in a loving way. Somehow their use of God's names as swear words made John miss his mother a lot.

'Dear Father in heaven,' he would begin some nights, before his father barged into their cabin, 'hear my prayer.'

Then he would try to remember the prayers his mother taught him, but that became harder and harder to do as his mind was full up with the things he was seeing and hearing.

'It's great to be on dry land!' John told his Aveley friends, when he visited home several months later.

They were on their way to school, and he was going for a ride.

'It's alright for some!' his red-headed friend laughed. 'The rest of us have to study. See you later!'

John tugged his horse's reins, dug in his heels, and the animal moved on. They walked the lanes round the village, John wanting to see if there were any changes in the months he'd been away. Then they went into the woods. John hoped to see some red squirrels, and he was not disappointed. One ran from branch to branch just above him.

'We don't have things like that at sea,' he told the horse. 'It's all fish there, and there aren't any horse-fish or squirrel-fish between here and the Mediterranean.'

The horse cantered right through the wood then along a lane where the hedge had just been cut. Suddenly something frightened the horse and it jumped and bucked all over the place. John, who had been relaxed in the saddle, was thrown. He landed just inches from the newly-cut hedge with its razor-sharp stakes. The boy sat up and, looking around, saw how near he had come to being very badly hurt indeed, perhaps even killed. Had he landed on the hedge the stakes could have done just that.

By then the horse had calmed down and, after walking alongside it for a while John remounted, and took the journey home slowly.

'What would have happened if I'd been killed there?' he asked himself, as they walked. 'Would I have seen Mum in heaven?'

Then he thought of the terrible things he had heard the sailors say, and of the things he had said himself.

'Maybe I'd not go to heaven?' he thought aloud, shocked at the very idea.

The names of God he'd used as swear words came tumbling into his mind.

'There's no way I'll go to heaven,' he whispered to himself, pulling the horse to a halt to give him time to think.

'I'm going to have to change,' he decided, before nudging the horse into movement again. 'If I'm to go to heaven when I die I'll have to change. I'm going to start reading the Bible and saying my prayers.'

He thought of his mother and knew that was exactly what she would have wanted him to do. John did begin to read and to pray before going to sleep at night ... for a while. But he didn't keep it up. Occasionally things happened that made him start again, but it never lasted for any length of time.

Just over two years after his horse threw him, John was again on dry land, this time near London.

'Do you see that man-of-war out there?' one of his friends asked.

All the boys looked in the direction of the ship he was pointing to.

'Let's go out and visit it this afternoon,' John said.

The others agreed and arranged a time. But when the fourteen-year-old arrived the others were already well out in the Thames.

'They've gone without me!' he stamped his foot in a rage and swore.

Then John saw the boat beginning to list. He watched spellbound. His friends stopped rowing and tried to right the boat but they misjudged it. The boat keeled over and the boys were thrown into the Thames. The lad saw sailors from nearby boats jumping in to save his friends and he tried to count how many were hauled out the water. He was desperate with worry by the time the small rowing boats bringing his friends back pulled alongside. Then a huge wave of relief swept over him as he saw one, then another, then another climb unsteadily up the stone steps. But there was one missing!

John ran to where his soaking friends were, and he knew from their faces before they told him the news. One boy had drowned.

Feeling weak and sick, John shuddered from head to toe.

'That could have been me,' he said to himself. 'If they'd waited for me that could have been me.'

That night John once again prayed, and promised to pray every day.

While he was still devastated by what had happened, John received an invitation to his friend's funeral. The card had pictures of gravestones, skeletons, coffins and shrouds round the edge. And while it was gruesome, the funeral ceremony was even more so.

'Tell me about it,' one of his Aveley friends asked later, thinking it would help.

'There were black coaches drawn by black horses with fearful plumes attached to them,' John remembered. 'Everything was as black as night.'

For what seemed a long time John's mind and heart seemed black too. He couldn't rid himself of the horror of what had happened, or the wonder of the fact he was still alive.

'I have decided not to go back to sea,' Captain Newton told his son in 1742. John was then 17 years old.

'What does that mean for me?' the teenager asked. 'Will I stay on your ship?'

'It's no longer my ship,' his father said. 'And I've made other arrangements for you anyway.'

John waited to be told. He knew better than to rush the Captain.

'I've asked my friend, Joseph Manesty, to take you to Jamaica. You'll get work in a sugar plantation there and train to be a manager.'

The lad's head was in a spin.

'I don't know anything about Jamaica,' he said.

His father laughed. 'You soon will.'

'And I don't know anything about managing a sugar plantation.'

'You'll learn,' Captain Newton said. 'And you'll have plenty of time to do so as you're committed to being there for four or five years.'

'Without a trip home?' the boy asked.

'That's right.'

'Jamaica sounds all right,' John thought. 'No doubt I'll soon learn the work. And what does it matter about not coming home? Nobody here will miss me.'

A week before he was due to leave, when all the preparations had been made, John wondered what to do with himself.

'I want you to go to Maidstone on an errand,' Captain Newton told his son. 'It'll help pass the time till you go.'

The boy was happy to ride to Maidstone because things were awkward at home. As he rode an idea came into his mind.

'Maidstone is not far from where the Catletts stay,' he remembered, having recently had a letter from his mother's friend, Mrs. Catlett. 'I'll take an extra couple of days and go to see them. I'll still be home in plenty of time.'

But he wasn't. John got such a warm welcome that he didn't want to leave again. And there was another reason why he didn't want to leave, a much more important one. He had fallen in love with the Catlett's daughter, Mary, who was almost fourteen years old. John stayed so long that he missed his ship for Jamaica. In fact, he stayed with the Catletts for three weeks and told them lies to explain how he was able to do so.

'What do you mean by this?' Captain Newton stormed, when his son eventually arrived home. 'Are you determined to make a fool of me?'

But the Captain's anger burned out and he made arrangements for his son to join the crew of a ship bound for Venice. On this voyage John was just an ordinary sailor, not the Captain's son, not sleeping in the Captain's cabin and certainly not eating at the Captain's table. And, having promised himself to lead a good life for the sake of Mary Catlett, before long he was every bit as bad as the worst of the crew. He used Jesus' name as a swear word more often than he used it in prayer and, when he was on his own, even he blushed at some of the stories he heard and told. Once he had a dream that pricked his conscience so much that he hardly ate or slept for days. But the good effect of the dream only lasted as long as the resolutions he had often made in the past.

'This is the absolute pits!' John fumed, some time later. 'One day I'm doing a good job as a merchant seaman, then the next I'm assaulted by a hooligan who thinks that the way to get men to join the Royal Navy is to encourage them with ropes round their wrists! I tell you,' he announced to the others who had been press-ganged the same day as he was, 'as far as I'm concerned the King can come and sail his own ships. I'll be off *HMS Harwich* before he has time to take his crown off and polish it!'

'If the Royal Navy treated sailors better they'd not need to go out into the streets and "encourage" men aboard,' one of the men said.

'Encourage!' spat John. 'You call dragging a man aboard a boat encouragement!'

It was the end of the winter, and gales lashed the mouth of the Thames where *HMS Harwich* rode at anchor. For a month all the press-ganged sailors did was brave the icy winds and snow as they scraped the decks, the sides of the ship and the lower masts. And when a change in the weather brought freezing cold dry winds from Siberia, they painted what they had scraped. Their hands were blistered and calloused. Infected hacks just about drove them crazy. And there was no let-up of the misery when they finished work and went below. 350 men crewed *HMS Harwich* and the sailor's quarters were appallingly overcrowded.

'It's the smell that's worst,' John thought one night, as he tried to sleep. 'As soon as I come below I feel sick. This ship is disgusting.'

He was nearly asleep when he needed to rush to relieve himself. Men, disturbed by him getting up again, swore into the darkness.

'And the food is indescribable! I'll guarantee that I'm not the only one with an upset stomach tonight,' he thought to himself, as he made his way back between them. 'I don't think I'll ever feel well and warm and clean again.'

To take his mind off the horrors around him, John thought about Mary. But for once he couldn't picture her face; he was feeling so awful, so utterly miserable.

'Newton!' a voice rang out over the roar of the wind. 'You've to go to the Captain!'

John's heart filled with hope. He'd got a message to a Lieutenant that he was a Captain's son in the hope that he'd be made a midshipman rather than a pressed sailor. Then fear hit him. Had he been reported for what he'd been saying about *HMS Harwich* and its Captain? What the young man didn't know was that his father had also been in touch with Captain Cartaret.

'So your Captain Newton's son,' Cartaret said. 'And he's not too keen on your being a pressed sailor. Can't think why! I would have thought it might be the making of you.'

John didn't meet the man's eye.

'But I suppose,' the Captain went on, 'we'd better give you a position more fitted to your background. You'll serve *HMS Harwich* as a midshipman.'

John could hardly believe it. That night, as he lay in his slightly more comfortable quarters, he thought about Mary. He could ask her to marry him now that he was a midshipman! He had potential!

That could have been the beginning of better things

for John Newton had he not been a very stupid young man. Captain Cartaret was not impressed when, more than once, John was late back aboard from visits to Mary. And Mary's father was not impressed by her boyfriend. The Captain finally lost patience when John tried to jump ship. He was caught, returned to *HMS Harwich*, clapped in irons and demoted. So when some time later a ship came alongside and Captain Cartaret pressed two men from its crew for service on *HMS Harwich*, he was more than happy to see John Newton leave in exchange for one of them.

'I don't know what *The Pegasus* will be like,' the young man thought, as he went from one ship to the other, 'but it can't be any worse than the *Harwich*. And as nobody on board will know my father I can do what I like!'

Help! We're Sinking!

'So this is Captain Newton's son,' said Captain Penrose of *The Pegasus*. 'You were very keen to leave *HMS Harwich*.'

John, who was wondering what on earth he had to do to escape people who knew his father, did not give an explanation for leaving the Royal Navy. Captain Penrose, despite his suspicions, treated the young man kindly enough, but got no thanks for it.

'I've made up a song about Penrose,' John told the other sailors shortly after he went aboard.

'Let's hear it,' one man said. 'And we'll tell you what we think of it.'

John sang a very rude and crude song about the Captain who had taken him on board.

'That's going a bit far,' one man remarked.

But he was hardly heard over the laughter of the other sailors.

'Any more verses?' a young fellow yelled.

John smirked. 'I'm working on that!'

Six months later Captain Penrose died. By then they were in West Africa.

'I've had enough of the sea,' John decided, when he heard how the slave trade operated in that part of the world. 'There's money to be made in slaves and I'm going to make it.'

'How do you know so much about it?' someone asked.

'I've been talking to Amos Clow,' explained Newton.

'Keeping in with the passengers!' a sailor laughed. 'And one that owns part of *The Pegasus* too! You know how to pick them.'

Newton told them to be quiet. 'Clow says that he'll take me on.'

That was how John came to be standing on the shore watching *The Pegasus* set sail without him. And he didn't mind one little bit.

'I want to build a house on the largest of the Plantane islands,' Clow said to his new employee. 'And you'll help with the work.'

'Newton is coming with us,' he told his woman friend. Her name was PI.

She shook her head. 'I don't like him.'

Clow raised his eyebrows. 'That suits me,' he laughed. 'So long as you like me I don't care who you don't like.'

PI scowled and walked off.

John watched how the slave trade worked with a view to becoming a trader himself. Raids were made deep into the countryside and men, women and children captured. Tied together like animals, they were half led, half dragged to the coast, several dying on the way. Children were expected to keep up the same speed as their parents. If they were unable to do that, and nobody was fit to carry them, children were left in the jungle to die. Traders only chose people who looked strong and healthy because they sold for a better price. So if anyone sickened and proved to be weak they were abandoned with no food and no water. Slaves were seen as things not as people. And just as a thing can be thrown away if it is not fit to do a job, these people were discarded if they were thought to be unfit for sale. The young man John Newton saw some terrible things, and he did some terrible things too.

Some months later, just as Clow was about to leave on slave business, John became unwell.

'PI will look after you,' his boss said. 'You'll be better by the time I get back.'

But he did not get better. By the end of that week he was very unwell indeed.

'Water,' John moaned. 'I need water.'

But nobody came, because nobody heard. PI, who was bored of looking after John, just left him alone even though he could not get out of his bed!

As the hours crept past John became thirstier and thirstier until his lips cracked and his tongue seemed to fill his whole mouth.

'Shh,' a voice said in the dark of the evening. 'You need water.'

One of the slaves had realised what had happened and risked his life by bringing water. But for the kindness of the slave, John Newton would have died. When he was a little better he asked PI for food.

'You want food?' she sneered. 'Then take this.'

She handed him some leftover food on the plate from which she had eaten. He was so weak and so hungry that he dropped the plate. PI laughed and refused to give him any more.

'You need food,' a voice said in the darkness later that night. And a slave's hand held out enough to keep John alive.

His strength returned slowly until he was able to walk about. Then he sometimes had to pull up roots and eat them raw and in secret as PI would have punished him if she had found out. When Clow returned home John told him what had happened, and told him in front of PI.

'Would I do that to your friend?' PI said, when he challenged her. 'The man is a liar!'

Clow looked from one to the other, and believed what the woman said. That sowed seeds of doubt in Amos Clow's mind about John's honesty. On their next slave-gathering voyage together he had John locked on deck with only a pint of rice each time he had to leave the boat. Fortunately Newton was a fisherman and he very soon improvised a rod and line to catch something he could eat.

'Dear Father,' John wrote. 'This is the third letter I have written to you from here. I wonder if you got the other two. I have decided not to return to England unless you invite me to do so. But it might be that you can give me some assistance here as I am in a very poor condition. My clothes are now ragged and I live on the worst of food.' He stopped and stroked his quill pen. 'Will you reach, Father?' he asked, looking at the letter. 'And what will he say if you do?' Then he continued writing. 'With Clow's permission I am going to live with another trader, Mr. Williams. He has several factories and I hope soon to be helping manage one of them.'

The move to working for Mr. Williams was a good one. Before long John could afford decent clothes. And he began to put on a little of the weight he had lost.

In February 1747, a ship called *The Greyhound* arrived in West Africa. The Captain was a friend of Captain Newton, and he had been asked to look out for John on his voyage. When the two met, the young man was happily employed by Mr. Williams and not at all willing to head for home. But the Captain told a lie to encourage him to return. 'Your father told me that a relative had left you £400 a year,' he said, much to John's surprise. The young man was in two minds. Then he thought of Mary.

'If I have £400 a year I could ask her to marry me. That would be quite enough to live on.'

John went aboard and left West Africa behind him. It was almost a year later that *The Greyhound's* trading was done and they set sail for England.

Because he was not a working sailor but a passenger on the ship, time sometimes passed slowly. There were only a few books on board, but one of them was a Christian book that John read just to help pass the time. Something in it pricked his conscience and he began to wonder if, perhaps, what the book said was true.

'What's wrong?' he yelled in his sleep. Then jumping to his feet he discovered that the ship was listing from side to side in a very frightening way and that his cabin was swilling with water. A bloodcurdling scream came from the deck.

'We're sinking!' a terrified voice shouted over the noise of the storm.

John rushed up to the deck.

'Get a knife,' the Captain told him. 'Quick, man!'

As he dropped below for his knife a sailor climbed up past him and was immediately washed overboard.

'She's filling with water!'

'Man the pumps!'

'The timbers are giving way!'

'Bale for your very lives!'

Voices carried in the wind were caught on the way past. The ship was nearly full of water, and getting fuller. But the cargo of beeswax and wood was light and helped keep them afloat. For hours all hands fought the storm, and the fear of sinking kept everyone struggling to throw as much water back at the sea as the sea was throwing at *The Greyhound*.

John was still at the pumps at daybreak.

'Keep going men,' he shouted. 'In a day or two we'll

be laughing about this over a drink.'

But there was nothing to laugh about and the men thought the only drink they'd be having was sea water as they drowned.

Pumping till his arms ached, until his body ached, until even his mind ached, John did what he could to save the ship. Let off for a while, he braced himself against the gale, held hard to the rail and headed for the Captain. Looking around at the crew's mammoth efforts to save the ship, John said, 'If this will not do, the Lord have mercy on us.'

Leaving the Captain, he returned to the pump. And as he worked at it his mind raced. 'What mercy can there be for me?'

The hours passed and the storm raged. John was still toiling at a pump at noon, nine hours after he began. Nearly every wave that hit the side of the ship crashed over his head and threatened to send him flying. He would have gone overboard had he not been lashed to the deck with ropes.

'I can do no more,' he said soon afterwards, and sank to the deck.

'Move, man!' a sailor roared in his ear, 'I'll take over.'

Grabbing the handle of the pump the man worked for all he was worth while John crawled to the hatch and slid down. Lying on his bed he would gladly have died but for the doubt he had about what would have happened then.

'Newton!' yelled the Captain, just an hour later.

John struggled to his feet and made for the deck.

The Captain looked at him; both men were almost broken with exhaustion.

'You're not fit to pump. Go to the wheelhouse and keep her on course.'

With what seemed his last ounce of energy John fought the wind to the wheelhouse where he stayed until midnight while the rest of the crew wrestled with the sea.

While he held the ship on course, the exhausted young man had time to think.

'What if the Bible is true?' he wondered. 'If it's true, and if this ship goes down, then I'm done for!'

The Greyhound lurched. John's heart lurched with it.

'I've cursed and sworn worse than anyone, even using God's name as a swear-word. I've told horrible stories that made everyone blush but me.' He shuddered at the memory of some of the things he had done and at the thought that if there was a God he might just be about to meet him. He knew God would not be impressed.

'Is there any hope for me?' he asked himself.

And from somewhere away back in his memory, verses of the Bible came to his mind that told him there was hope, and that hope was in Jesus.

About six o'clock the next evening the ship was freed of water, and it seemed that they were safe.

John Newton prayed as he'd never prayed before. He didn't feel able to call God 'Father', he knew something had to happen before that could be true. Instead he just called out for help, not from a sinking ship, but from the possibility of spending forever in hell.

The following day, while he was thinking about these things, news spread round the ship that they were nearly out of food. Most had been washed away in the storm and what was left would last less than a week.

Five days later land was sighted.

'Have you ever seen anything more beautiful?' John asked a sailor, as they watched the sun rise over a row of islands.

The sailor nodded his head. 'I never thought I'd see the likes again.'

Eventually the ship arrived safely in Ireland. It was while it was there being refitted that John became convinced that he had put his trust in the Lord Jesus Christ and become a Christian. In May 1748 he arrived back in England.

Human Cargo

'I know you're only 23 years old, but I'm prepared to make you captain of one of my slave ships,' Captain Manesty told John. 'You've had experience of the slave trade in West Africa and sailing's in your blood. Apart from that you're Captain Newton's son, and I've known him for years.'

John shuffled his feet, unwilling to say 'yes', and not wanting to say 'no'.

'Well?' Manesty demanded. 'Are you up to it?'

That gave the young man the opening he needed.

'To be honest,' he told the Captain, 'I don't think I am yet. I'd rather do another voyage as Mate before taking charge of a ship.'

Manesty was impressed. 'You're a wise young man. And you'll make a better captain for waiting a while.'

John signed on as Mate on *The Brownlow* and made plans for the short time before it was due to sail.

'I must see Mary,' he told a friend. 'I wrote to her aunt asking if Mary was still single and I've not had a reply, so this might be a useless journey. But I've got to go.'

When John arrived at the Catletts he discovered that Mary was not married and that he was still very much in love with her.

'May I ask you something?' he said towards the end of his visit to her home.

She nodded, but John was totally tongue-tied. He wanted to ask her to marry him, but the words were stuck in his mouth and wouldn't come out.

Mary waited. John grabbed the first words he could find. 'May I write you a letter?' he asked, furious that he hadn't had the courage to say what he really wanted to say.

She agreed he could. And when the letter came, Mary was left in no doubt what John Newton felt for her.

The Brownlow eventually set sail to John's old haunts in West Africa on a slave-gathering trip. But first they had to get there and the Mate had plenty of time on his hands. Because he was hoping soon to be a captain and a married man, he decided to educate himself, and so read as much as time allowed. He took up Latin again and studied it hard. Unfortunately he also took up some of the sins he had stopped committing, and it took another serious illness to make him realise what he was allowing to happen.

'A few weeks should see us ready to sail to the West Indies,' the Captain told John, after they had been gathering slaves for seven months.

His Mate agreed. 'We should make a handsome profit on them when we get there. The men are among the strongest I've seen and the women are not a bad lot either.'

'Thankfully there hasn't been too much illness among them.'

'All it takes is for measles or some other such thing to weaken them and much of the profit sinks to the bottom of the sea,' commented John.

'There's a fine line,' the Captain said, 'between stuffing the hold full of slaves so that if we lose some during the voyage there are still plenty to sell, and not taking so many in the hope that the ones we take will be in better condition when we arrive in Jamaica.'

'I've noticed a few that are beginning to look poorly,' the Mate pointed out. 'I think we should leave them behind in case they are sickening for something that will spread through them all.'

The Captain nodded. 'You've got a good business head. We could leave them working in the lime plantations here, and if they survive till we come back for the next lot we can take them with us then.'

'Raise the anchor!' the Captain called, four weeks later.

The ships hold was full of slaves: men, women and children. And the noise was horrendous. As they left port there was a wailing that could be heard on land. Although the weather was fair for the first part of the journey, it started to get rough before they were many days out.

'I can smell vomit every time I go near the ladder down to the hold,' John said to one of the sailors.

'Just be glad you're not down there with the slaves,' the sailor replied. 'They are packed hard by each other, and when one is sick those around him can't move to avoid it. And I don't think it's just seasickness, I reckon some disease is doing the rounds.'

The Captain grimaced. 'That's not good news,' he said. 'We don't want to lose more than we can help.'

As he spoke, two young sailors brought the body of a teenage slave out of the hold.

'He's the first to die,' one of them told the Captain, 'but he won't be the last.'

The body was fed to the sea, and nobody who loved the lad was there to see it go. The next overboard was a new baby. She was born in the hold and, though she lived a few hours, she had not one single breath of fresh air in her tiny lungs. It was only days later that her mother died of an infection and joined her baby in the wide ocean.

'Several of the slaves have stopped eating,' John was told by the Captain. 'I've ordered the men to put them in neck collars and use the mouth openers.'

Suddenly John's memory took him back to when he was six years old, and the day the boys in Little Bear Quay explained what neck collars and mouth openers were for.

The Captain was still speaking. '.... and when you're in charge of your own slave ship remember not to let them off with anything. Think what would happen if things got out of hand down there, you could have slaves over-running the ship. They need to be kept down, and if they don't keep the rules they're chained. If they don't eat they're force-fed. And if they die they are quickly put overboard to stop the spread of disease.'

'It's not a nice business,' John commented.

'It's maybe not the nicest, but it pays well,' laughed the Captain. 'And don't you be getting sentimental about it. They are slaves, remember, not people like you and me.'

Newton thought about the money he was earning and decided it was all worthwhile.

'I'll be right glad to get this lot off my hands,' the Captain told him, as they watched their cargo of slaves being unloaded at Charlestown in Carolina, their route having been changed.

'Look at them,' John said. 'You'd never know they were the strong healthy slaves we got in West Africa.'

'But they're a lot better than some I've seen,' retorted the Captain. 'And thanks to them our pockets will be rattling with gold by tonight.'

John grinned, and felt the empty space in his pockets where the gold would be.

'I'm going to have a look around.'

After some hours exploring Charlestown, John found his way to the slave market. It was the sound of crying and wailing that took him there. He watched as what looked like husbands and wives were bought by different masters and taken away in opposite directions. And he heard the screams of children being sold separately from their parents, and the loud moans of their mothers as they went, moans that seemed to come from deep inside them. And, having checked that the sale prices were good, John headed back to *The Brownlow*. But he didn't stay. The sailors were cleaning out the hold and the smell was utterly vile. He decided to take a walk through the grander parts of Charlestown to get away from it all.

Within a few months *The Brownlow* was back in Liverpool. Manesty was there to meet it and to promise John a captaincy for the next sailing season. John felt ready to accept, but he had other things on his mind. As soon as was possible and proper he proposed to Mary Catlett. At first she turned him down. The next time she forbade him to raise the subject again. And the third time Mary accepted. Two weeks later, on 12th February 1750, they were married in Rochester. For three months they lived with Mary's parents and John showed Mary the things he'd discovered about the countryside. Her dog, Fancy, thought John was the best thing that had ever arrived in the Catlett home because he took her for such long walks!

'There's a letter for you,' Mrs. Catlett said to John one day.

He tore it open and read in silence.

'It's from Captain Manesty,' John told his wife. Then he grinned from ear to ear. 'And I've some news for you. You're no longer married to plain Mr. Newton, I'm a Captain now!'

It took a moment for Mary to realise what he was

saying. Then she clapped her hands in excitement.

'You mean you've got your own ship?' she asked.

John nodded. 'That's right. I'm Captain Newton of *The Duke of Argyle*. That's the good news. The bad news is that I've to go to Liverpool to see her fitted out.'

'And then?' Mary's smile had faded and she looked very serious.

'And then,' her husband told her, 'I'll be leaving for West Africa. And that, I'm afraid, is what our married life is going to be like.'

Mary held him close, burying her face in his woollen sailor's jersey so that he could not see the tears that were threatening to fall.

'So this is *The Duke of Argyle*,' John thought, as he arrived at the quay in Liverpool, 'all hundred and fifty tonnes of her. She's an old girl too. I only hope she holds together long enough to get me back to Mary.'

But from the time he arrived in the port his days were so full that there was little time to think about anything else but getting his ship ready to sail.

'What's that noise?' he asked the Mate one day.

'It's the carpenter, Cap'n,' the man answered. 'He's down in the hold building the barriers to keep the slaves in.'

'Tell him not to hammer too hard or he'll knock the ship apart!'

The Mate grinned. 'She's seen better days right enough.'

'Is everything aboard?' the Captain asked.

'The shackles, chains, iron collars and mouth openers are all below. And the food for the ship's company is there too. All we're waiting for is the pulped beans for the slaves.'

'See to it,' John told the Mate. 'And be quick about it. The weather's been set fair for days and it won't last much longer. It's time Liverpool was disappearing in the distance behind us.'

On the 10th August, 1750, John was getting ready to set sail. Even though he was rushed off his feet in the last minute preparations before sailing he found some time to write a brief letter to Mary, 'There is not much time, my dear Mary, but I'll send a letter from our first port or by a passing ship if we meet one that's making for England. Don't be alarmed if you don't hear from me for months. Remember, you're a Captain's wife now and that is how it will be. Pray for me and I'll pray for you. Your loving husband, John. Note. Remember to look at the North Star every clear night at the time we agreed, then we might be looking at it together."

Sending the letter on its way John set to work with last minute checks before the ship, *The Duke of Argyle*, set sail. He checked to make sure that all the ship's company was present and correct: thirty men in total including three Mates, a carpenter and a doctor. 'What's the condition of the ship?' he asked one of the Mates.

'It's a very old vessel, Captain - and a bit crazy, if I may say so. The carpenter's going to have his work cut out on this voyage.'

John nodded. 'Yes, it's up to him to keep her together until we all get home again! Are the compartments in the hold completed yet?'

'Aye, Cap'n. The slave compartments are ready - one each for men, boys and women. He's finishing off the shelves in each compartment so that the slaves can lie in rows. They'll look just like that nice little row of books you have in your cabin,' the Mate chuckled.

'What about the shackles?' John continued. 'We must make sure that they have no opportunity for escape.'

'Well, the right hand and foot of one slave is going to be chained to the left hand and foot of the next one and so on, so they will all be held in long rows. The carpenter has to put ringbolts in the hold and on deck too. In the hold the last slaves in each row are going to be shacked to the ringbolts. And, because in good weather we bring them on deck for the air, he needs to put ringbolts on the deck to hold them secure there.'

John nodded. It was just as it should be. The ship was ready. *The Duke of Argyle* left Liverpool the next morning. Three days later John took a leather-bound book from a shelf in his cabin. Opening it at the first page, he wrote,

> *Journal*
> *Kept on board The Duke of Argyle*
> *from Liverpool to Africa*
> *Commenced the 14th August, 1750.*

Below that he added, in Latin, a verse from Psalm 107.

'They that go down to the sea in ships, that do business in great waters; They see the works of the Lord, and his wonders in the deep.'

Aye, Aye, Captain Newton

When *The Duke of Argyle* eventually reached West Africa, John Newton set about the business of buying slaves. After some weeks of trading, he read over his log.

'Longboat returned with eleven slaves: three men, one woman, two older boys, two younger boys and three undersized girls.'

'Bought two small girls. Sent the steward ashore again to purchase a woman slave and he brought her in the evening. She is number 46. She cost 65 bars even though she has a very bad mouth. I think I could have bought her cheaper myself.'

'Today I got a woman slave from Captain Williams in exchange for three small boys and a girl.'

'Today I buried a fine woman slave, number eleven. She had been ill for some time but I didn't realise her life was in danger. Because she was infectious we scraped the rooms and smoked the ship with tar, tobacco and brimstone for two hours then had it washed with vinegar.'

John turned the page and his face became very serious.

'The longboat returned in a miserable condition

they having buried one of the people. The Mate and the three others on board are sick, two of them dangerously. The boat was laden with eleven slaves. They were one man, two women, five sizeable girls, one boy and two small girls. It also brought 400 lbs of rice and other stores.'

He read on.

'Close dirty weather; wind down the coast and a great sea tumbling in. At 2 a.m. our carpenter died, the third member of the ship's company to die in three weeks and another four are very ill. Put a slave boy ashore today. He was infectious. Then another of the crew took the same thing. We now have five whites very ill.'

'Sent the Mate ashore to see if fresh air and a good diet would help him. He died.'

He closed the book. 'I've no time to read,' John said. 'There's work to be done.'

Striding across the deck, he met one of the two remaining Mates.

'We sail with tomorrow's tide,' he said. 'There are 175 slaves in the hold and we need to be off.'

The Mate nodded grimly. 'The first ships to arrive always get the best prices for slaves. So even though there are 175 of them and less than 25 of us we'll weigh anchor and head out to sea. I just wish the 25 were all fit; some of them are still very ill.'

'I know that,' Captain Newton said. 'It's to be hoped they'll soon recover.'

Not all did, and many slaves died as they crossed the South Atlantic Ocean. But those that were left sold for a fair price.

Sitting in the Captain's cabin, John counted the gold on his desk and worked out what to buy with it. 'I need to chose carefully,' he thought, 'and get things that will sell for a good price back in England.'

There was a crash down below in the hold.

'This is one bit of the job I just hate,' moaned John. 'The crew is clearing the hold now that the slaves are ashore, and the stench gets worse by the hour. It's seeping up through the floor into my cabin and there's nowhere free of it. Even on deck you can't avoid it as they bring bucket after bucket after dripping bucket of refuse up and out. But there's no point in fumigating the hold until the last of the muck is scraped off.'

He tried to concentrate on the goods he would buy, but his stomach was heaving.

'I'll need to go ashore,' he decided. 'I can't take any more.'

A sailor lowered a small rowing boat from the side of the ship and Newton climbed down into it.

'Are you all right?' the sailor asked, as he rowed for the quay.

Newton nodded, not sure if the contents of his stomach were going to reach the quay or not.

'Nasty business, clearing the hold,' the sailor commented, then turned away to save his Captain's embarrassment.

By the time the ship was loaded with its new cargo, the crew could hardly wait to set sail for home.

'My dear Mary,' John wrote, as he began that day's instalment of the letter he wrote every night to his wife, 'we are loaded and ready to go. We've picked up a mixed cargo, and one that won't sicken or die on us. Tomorrow we set sail for home. I can't tell you how much I'm looking forward to seeing you. There's a clear sky tonight and it's "our appointed time" so I'm going to go and look at the North Star in the hope that you are looking at it too. In a few months we'll stand side by side and look at it together. That day cannot come quickly enough for me.'

Liverpool docks came clearly into view as *The Duke of Argyle* lowered sail and was piloted in. If the sailors had not had a lot to do they would have been hanging over the side of the ship watching to see if anyone they knew was there to see them come in.

'Only 16 of the crew of 30 that set out with us are still alive,' John said to the Mate. 'That's 14 widows to be told, and probably more than 40 children who'll never see their fathers again.'

'It's a dirty business' the Mate agreed. 'And there's no easy way of doing it.'

Setting his sights on the dockside, Newton wondered how to begin telling the bad news. 'It has to be done,' he thought. 'It could have been me.'

* * *

'Newton, my man!' Captain Manesty said, when they met soon afterwards. 'I heard you were home and that your voyage was successful.'

'To a point.' John was guarded in his response.

Manesty looked puzzled. 'You're back,' he laughed. 'Your pockets are full. What more do you want?'

John swallowed and decided to say what was on his mind.

'I said the voyage was successful to a point,' he began. 'And as you say we're home again. But we might not have been. Have you any idea the state *The Duke of Argyle* is in? When the ship's carpenter died of fever I thought we might lose the boat!'

'What do you mean?' asked Manesty.

'She's held together by habit!' *The Duke's* Captain explained. The carpenter spent almost as much time patching her up as preparing to take the slaves on board. And it's only because he did a good job that the ship didn't go to the bottom of the ocean like the poor man himself.'

Captain Manesty coughed. 'Well, yes,' he agreed. 'She's an old girl, and I agree she needs replacing. Do you think she's fit for one more voyage.'

John stood his ground. 'Not with me as her captain!'

Manesty rubbed his chin. He was deep in thought and the younger man didn't know what he was thinking.

'All right then,' the ship's owner said. 'We'll have a new ship built and you'll be her first Captain. How does that sound.'

John smiled. 'That sounds good to me,' he laughed. 'It sounds really good.'

'It would take time to build a new ship,' he thought, 'time I can spend with Mary.'

In April 1752, *The African* was ready for launching. Once again a letter arrived from Captain Manesty, this one telling him when the launch would be and ordering him to be there.

'What a noise and fuss and great spending of money,' John decided after the launch. 'It was more than a little over the top, and people who should have known better were being really silly.'

Something about the launch of his new ship bothered him.

'Nobody seemed in the least interested in asking God to keep us safe at sea,' he wrote to Mary. 'And if he doesn't do that the grandest vessel in the world could shatter in the first storm that hit her. I'm going to ask the Christians here in Liverpool to pray for *The African* as we set sail for Africa. That will be about midsummer and we should be away for around a year. I think *The African* will be a bit like me, slow and steady rather than quick in the water.'

'There will be prayer at the start of each day on *The African*,' Newton told his new Mate.

'There usually is when it's convenient,' agreed the Mate.

The Captain shook his head. 'Not only when it's convenient; there will be prayer every day. For goodness sake, man, do you not think we need God's help at sea?'

Blushing beneath his dark brown tan the Mate agreed. Newton saw the shocked expression and realised that the crew would find some differences working under a Christian captain.

Newton carried on, 'And on Sundays all the ship's company will meet for worship.'

'All?'

'All,' John said firmly. 'And I'm working on a collection of prayers suitable for sailors.'

'That'll be interesting,' the other man commented. Newton looked at the Mate's smirking face and thought, 'He's probably wondering why sailors needed a set of prayers at all. I can imagine the comments he'll make to the other sailors "Looks like we're sailing a church boys. The Captain will be writing a collection of suitable prayers for the slaves next!" Another smirk from the Mate brought a sharp response from Newton, 'Something amusing you?' the Captain asked.

'No, Cap'n,' mumbled the other man. 'Not at all, Sir.'

If the ship's company thought John was a soft mark and would let them off with anything because he was a Christian, they were mistaken. Some of them found that out for themselves, as the Captain recorded in the ship's journal.

'Discovered that John Cooper and James Allen had drained ale from a cask for their own use. After hiding the ale where they could find it when they wanted it, they refilled the cask with water. I put them in irons and ordered that Allen should have 11 lashes and Cooper 17, he being an officer.'

Sometimes trouble came from down in the hold where the human cargo was incarcerated.

'By God's goodness,' the Captain recorded, 'I discovered that some slaves were forming a plot for insurrection. I surprised two of them trying to get their irons off. On questioning three boy slaves I was led to unearth a hoard of knives, stone shot and a chisel. On investigation I discovered there were eight involved, four men and four boys. I put the boys in irons and thumbscrews ....'

Captain Newton's firmness paid off, especially on his second voyage on *The African*.

'Did you hear the news?' a docker said, after the ship arrived back in Liverpool in August 1754.

'What's wrong?' his companion asked.

'Nothing's wrong!' laughed the docker. 'Nothing at all. It was good news I heard. Apparently *The African* has arrived back with no loss of life at all.'

His friend stopped what he was doing.

'You mean all the crew survived the voyage?'

'Aye. That's just what I mean. And that's not all!'

'You can't better that,' his friend commented.

'Oh yes you can,' the docker said. 'The whole cargo of slaves survived too. Every man, woman and child survived to be sold. Newton must have made a lot on that voyage.'

The other man shook his head. 'I don't believe you,' he snorted. 'That's just not possible!'

'Excuse me,' a woman's voice said from behind them.

They both swung round.

'My name's Mrs. Newton,' the woman said. 'I came up to Liverpool to meet my husband, Captain Newton of *The African*, and I'd like to confirm what your friend has just told you. The ship sailed with no loss of life, either crew or slave.'

'Captain Manesty is having a faster ship fitted for me,' John told his wife a short time later. 'He was so pleased with my last voyage.'

Mary smiled. 'I'm not surprised. But you'll be hard-pressed to do as well next time. I suppose the only way you could improve would be if some of the female slaves had babies at sea and you ended the voyage with more than you started with!'

'That's a good one!' John laughed. 'That's a really good one!'

* * *

Two days before John's next ship, *The Bee*, was due to sail, a man arrived in Manesty's office.

'What's wrong?' the Captain asked, seeing his visitor's anxious expression.

'It's Captain Newton,' the sailor said. 'He's had a seizure.'

Manesty was on his feet. 'Tell me exactly what happened,' he demanded.

The sailor told the story. 'He was just doing his usual work when he started twitching. Then he fell over and wrenched back and fro, with his eyes rolling to the top of his head. When his body fell quiet we thought he was dead. For a whole hour he lay there, alive and breathing but never moving at all, not at all.'

The sailor stopped for breath.

'Go on, man,' the Captain urged.

'Then Mr. Newton seemed to wake up and he was quite himself again apart from a headache and feeling dizzy.'

'Has a doctor seen him?'

'There's one with him now,' the sailor concluded.

The following day, just 24 hours before *The Bee* was due to set sail, Captain John Newton resigned his command of the ship. He was not quite 30 years old.

'How am I to provide for Mary?' he asked himself, as he watched *The Bee* being piloted out the following day. 'What can a young retired sea captain who takes seizures do for a living?'

Surveying the Tides

'It's good to be ashore,' John told his wife, as they walked along a street in Basseterre, 'but I don't know what kind of shore job a seaman like me will find to do.'

Mary took his arm. 'I've no doubt that something will come up. Meanwhile, I'm just grateful to have you home and to have you well.'

'That seizure was a strange thing,' he commented, 'and the timing of it too.'

'Just be grateful that it happened when it did,' Mary said. 'You could have been in the middle of the Atlantic.'

They walked in silence for a few minutes before John spoke again. 'It's almost as though God stopped me from going on *The Bee*. But why would he do that?'

'Maybe he wanted you out of the slave trade.'

The Newtons stopped and sat down on a wall by the side of the road.

'You were never happy about me trading slaves, were you?' John asked.

Mary shook her head. 'It upset me to think of those poor souls taken away from their families and sold to men who would work them to death.'

'But there's another side to it,' he pointed out. 'In

their African villages these people would never have heard about the Lord. But when they went to America or the West Indies they often started going to church. In fact, some slave masters insisted they went to church every Sunday. When I was in Carolina I heard slaves singing hymns.'

'Were they happy hymns?' his wife asked.

'What do you mean?'

'I think those poor souls must have felt like the Jews when they were exiled from their own land. And remember how sad some of the psalms are, that talk about those days.'

John started singing the words of a psalm softly, as though to himself,

'By Babel's streams we sat and wept,
when Sion we thought on.
In midst thereof we hanged our harps
The willow-trees upon.
For there a song required they,
Who did us captive bring:
Our spoilers called for mirth, and said.
A song of Sion sing.'

After what seemed a very long silence he got to his feet. 'It's time we were making our way home,' he said.

In August 1755, just nine months after his one and only seizure, John Newton was back in Liverpool to take up a job within the Customs Service. His title was Tide Surveyor.

The day after he started work there he wrote to Mary, who was down south in London and very unwell.

'My work is in a two week cycle. On week one I visit the ships that arrive with the tide. The other week I inspect vessels in the docks. The week I visit the ships that arrive will be very hard work as they come in day and night depending on the tides. Inspecting the ones in docks is much easier. My office is comfortable, with a fire to keep me warm and a candle to light my work. Some fifty or sixty people work under me. Today is very windy.'

And when he wrote again at the end of the week he told his wife about his first catch.

'When ships come in captains declare the cargo and my men check that they are not carrying anything over and above what they declare. Today we found one that was. As well as what was on the Captain's sheet, we found 1704 pounds of tobacco, 66 gallons of rum, 17 gallons of cherry brandy, 31 cases of snuff, and a considerable amount of coffee. The man would have made a fortune on that had we not found it! As it is, I do very well out of it. Things I find are seized and condemned and I get half of the value. That should buy you a new gown next time you need one. I pray that you'll soon be well enough to be thinking of gowns and such things.'

A month after John Newton started work as a Tide Surveyor, a famous preacher visited Liverpool. John had heard George Whitefield in London and he really wanted to hear him preach again.

'I'm glad this is my week for inspecting ships in the docks,' he thought. 'That'll give me time to hear Mr. Whitefield. I'll be able to go to the open-air service at 5 o'clock in the morning in St. Thomas's Square. And I may be able to get back to hear him again in the evening.'

Things worked out better than John planned. He was able to get to both open-air services and also see George Whitefield personally in the afternoon. Newton asked his landlady if she would like to come to hear the preacher. At first she would not, but she eventually went along. She was so impressed that she agreed to ask Mr. Whitefield back for dinner.

'My dear Mary, I learned such a lot from that good man,' John wrote by candlelight that evening. 'But I just wish you had been there to hear him. I long for you to be well enough to join me here in Liverpool.'

He blew out the candle and went to bed. But it was a very long time before he fell asleep as all sorts of things were buzzing around in his head, especially the words of one of the Liverpool dockers who had called him Young Mr. Whitefield. 'I want to tell people about Jesus,' he thought, as he nodded off, 'but I'm not sure that I could ever stand up and preach.'

Liverpool was usually a peaceful place, but when war broke out with France and Spain in 1756, things became a little fraught.

'I hear the press-gangs are out these nights,' a sailor told John one day.

A shudder went down John's spine as he remembered when he'd been pressed into the king's service.

'I'm sure they are,' he replied. 'The king will be needing all the men he can get to man the ships of the Royal Navy. And as conditions are still appalling aboard his ships, I've no doubt he'll have to get his men by foul means rather than fair.'

'What on earth!' Newton said, as he went into the Watch House one Thursday soon afterwards.

The place looked as though a battle had been fought in it. 'What's happened here?' he asked his clerk.

'Remember the forty men who were press-ganged and taken aboard *The Bolton*?' the lad began.

'Yes,' Newton said. 'They mutinied, killed a Mate, and made for the shore on Sunday. As far as I know most are hiding in various houses in the town though some have been recaptured. But what's that got to do with this mess?'

The lad continued with his story. 'Last night some Navy men chased one of the deserters in here. But a mob gathered, all of them on the deserter's side. They fought the sailors, broke into the Watch House and let the fellow free!'

'Was anyone hurt?'

'The keeper of the watch had some ribs broken,' the lad admitted. 'But I'm still glad the sailor got away.'

Newton nodded his head. 'I'm sure he is too.'

'What ship is that in the distance?' one Customs man asked another.

His colleague raised his telescope and settled his sights on the ship.

'If I'm not mistaken it's *The Golden Lion*.'

Newton, who had been sitting at his desk writing, raised his head.

'*The Golden Lion*, did you say? That's Manesty's ship back from the Greenland Whale Fishery. I'll let him know it's coming.'

'At least her crew is safe from the press-gangs,' John's clerk said. 'Because whaling is so important they are exempt from service in the Navy.'

John watched the ship nearing port.

'What's going on?' he said, as four boat-loads of Navy men from *The Vengeance* rowed towards *The Golden Lion*.

'What is it?' two Customs officers asked together.

With the telescope to his eye, John gave a running commentary.

'They've boarded her but the ship's company is up in arms. Some of them are brandishing blubber knives and harpoons! The Navy men look as though they're going to put up a fight. No, no … the crew are forcing them to the rail. If they don't get off quickly they'll be pushed into the sea!'

'What's happening now?' the young clerk asked,

desperate to be in on the action.

'Well! Well!' laughed Newton, 'the King's brave men have turned tail and they're clambering down into their boats. They can't get away quick enough!'

'Serves them right!' the clerk said.

They were just settling back to work when a noise made them jump.

Newton was out the door with his telescope in less time that it takes to tell.

'This I don't believe,' he said. '*The Vengeance* is opening fire on *The Golden Lion*!'

Captain Manesty's ship cut and ran from the man-of-war. Her sails, rigging and mizzen stay were badly damaged by the nine-pound shots that crashed into her side.

The following day, when Manesty's crew went to have their protection from press-ganging renewed, the Navy men followed them to the Customs House. In the fight that followed, five of *The Golden Lion's* sailors were captured for the king. The Captain was taken too, but he was released later.

'It was sad to see these men being hauled off,' John said to his wife. 'So many of them will be killed in this war and their women and children left destitute. The king is quick to take men into his service, but not to help their families.'

Mary agreed, 'I've been praying for the wives and children. But that seems such a little thing to do.'

'Not at all! Prayer is the biggest of all things we

can do for them because it pleads for the help of the King of Kings.'

'I've not thought about it in that way before,' the woman pondered. 'You're quite right, and I'll pray all the more for them.'

'Are you nervous?' Mary asked her husband, as he prepared to take family worship for the Catletts for the first time. It was towards the end of 1756.

'It's a strange thing,' he replied. 'I've taken services for my ship's crew for years, but this has a very different feel about it.'

'What are you going to speak about?'

John opened his Bible at Matthew 5. 'My text is from the Sermon on the Mount.'

Nothing like this had ever happened in the Catletts home before. Mary deliberately didn't look around the room as her husband was speaking because she was unsure how her family was responding. She bit her lip when he seemed to be stumbling over his words, but he picked up again and continued.

'Let us pray,' Mary heard him say, and she slid to her knees thankfully.

Soon afterwards a friend suggested that John should become a preacher. But he remembered back to his days of using God's name as a swear word and wondered if God could ever make a preacher of someone who had done that. Although he didn't see himself as a preacher, he studied Hebrew and Greek in order that he could read the Old and New Testaments in the languages in which they were written. While he might not be a preacher of God's Word, he would certainly be a good student of the Bible.

Thoughts of the ministry would not leave John alone. So he kept the day of his 33rd birthday entirely free and spent the whole day thinking about his future. Did God want him to be a preacher? What kind of preacher would he be? Was he able for the job? From 6am till 5pm, he remained alone. By the time be joined Mary for their evening meal, he had settled in his mind that God might be calling him to the ministry. All that remained was for the church to agree and ordain him.

All Change!

Things continued much as usual in the Newtons' lives. John worked as a Customs Officer and Mary looked after him when she was able, and rested when she was not. Her health was not very good at all.

'It's time I left for work,' he said every morning, and every morning his wife smiled.

'You have plenty of time. Have you ever been late for anything?'

'I suppose it's my training,' he admitted, 'but I don't like being late and I don't like when others are late either.'

His wife grinned mischievously.

'I'll make sure the maid has your meal ready on the dot of dinner-time.'

Chuckling, he kissed her and left for the Watch House.

Several times that day he smiled at what had been said, especially when he found himself sitting at his desk, holding his watch in front of him, so that he could leave at the exact time his boatmen would arrive to take him to inspect a vessel.

'Dead on time!' the boatmen said to each other. 'Mr. Newton's never late.'

John heard what they said as he climbed aboard.

'I was late once,' he told them. 'And it was God who kept me late.'

'It certainly was,' one of the boatmen remembered.

As the other boatman was new and didn't know the story, his friend went on and told him what had happened.

'Once Mr. Newton was late and we had to wait for him quite some time. When he eventually arrived we set out for the ship. But we weren't far from shore when the ship we were going to blew up!'

Newton shook his head at the memory.

'Everyone on board was killed,' he said. 'And I would have been killed too if I'd been aboard. God was good to me that day.'

The older boatman agreed. 'He was good to me too. If this little boat had been lying beside the ship we would have gone into the air with her and then we'd have joined her on the seabed.'

'I'll just have to be patient,' John often told himself as he worked at the docks. 'If God wants me to be a minister he'll show me in his own good time.'

'Mr. Newton,' one of his men gasped, as he ran into the Watch House. 'There's a very strange looking ship some way out.'

Within minutes John was up and ready to go.

'Come on!' he called. 'Let's see what she's carrying.'

Newton boarded and searched the 13 tonne boat.

'Where's your cargo list?' he asked the Captain.

The man shuffled his feet.

'I don't rightly know,' he said aggressively. 'And I don't know what business it is of yours.'

John ignored that comment and began the search.

'Well, Mary, I have a story to tell you over dinner,' he said, when he arrived home that evening.

'I hope it's a good one,' she commented.

'You'll enjoy it.'

John was in a teasing mood and decided to keep his wife wondering what the story was about. He said he'd tell her while they were eating their dinner. When they sat down at the table, he looked at his wife for a long time.

'Would you like a wig?' he enquired eventually.

She put her cutlery down.

'What are you talking about?' she asked, patting her hair into place.

'I just wondered if you'd like a wig.'

'Why would I want a wig? I've a good head of hair!'

He laughed aloud.

'Today I captured a smugglers' ship and confiscated its cargo. What do you think was on board?'

Mary looked puzzled.

'Alcohol, tobacco, silk, coffee ... the usual things?'

'No,' he laughed. 'Try again.'

'I have no idea. You'll have to tell me.'

John laid down his spoon. 'It had a whole mixture of things, probably most of them stolen. But it also had the most unusual cargo I've come across so far.'

'What was that?' his wife asked.

'It was 10 pounds weight of human hair!'

Mary shuddered. 'And you're offering me some of it for a wig!'

Grinning, John admitted that he'd only been joking.

It was six years after John had felt called to the ministry that God opened the way for him to be ordained. By then he was 39 years old and his wife 35. That meant big changes as the Newtons left Liverpool for Olney in the Midlands.

One of the things Mary packed was the box of letters that John had sent her while he was at sea.

'Dear Father and Mother,' Mary wrote not long after arriving in Olney. 'As you asked me to write and tell you about this place, that's just what I'm going to do. At least, I'll tell you about the people because it is they who are interesting. The place is just a big industrial town. Almost every woman here is a lace-maker. They work in their own homes, often for ten hours a day. Many of the men help with their wives' work after their own day's work is done. And the children work too, filling the bobbins for their mothers. By the time children are three or four years old they are threading bobbins, setting pins and turning the bobbin-wheel. An extraordinary number of the women have damaged their eyesight by making lace by candlelight in the long winter evenings, especially as they have only one candle between three or four workers. And I understand that because coal is so expensive they keep themselves warm by filling an earthenware pot with hot ashes and putting it under their feet. They must suffer terribly from chilblains!'

Mary put her quill down. She had heard her husband come in and went to help him off with his coat.

Before many months had passed the Newtons felt quite at home in Olney, and the people seemed quite at home with them.

'I feel welcome wherever I go,' John told their maid, as she served his dinner one day.

'I'm sure you are, Mr. Newton,' she replied. 'I hear that you visit the women when they are working and talk, read and pray with them.'

'Yes,' he agreed. 'I don't keep them from their work though. They don't stop while we talk and when I'm reading, though they do when we pray.'

'And you have them singing too, I hear.'

John smiled. 'Yes, I have them singing hymns rather than some of their lace-making songs.'

'Singing to the bobbins is as old as lace-making,' the maid explained. 'But there's nothing to stop them singing to the Lord instead.'

'I couldn't put it better myself,' he said, as she turned to go into the kitchen.

'My heart goes out to these children,' Mary told her husband. 'They work with their mothers, and when they're not working they're out in the streets whatever the weather.'

'Have you listened to the words of their games?' he asked.

'I did once, and wished I hadn't.'

'They're a rough lot on the outside, but underneath they are just little children. I've been wondering what I could do for them.'

'But you've no experience of children,' his wife protested.

'It's true that we don't have any of our own but I have had experience of children, experience that I'd rather forget.'

Mary noticed that her husband's face had saddened.

'Yes, I suppose you do,' she agreed, thinking of the slave children John had bought and sold. 'I suppose you do.'

'Would you like me to tell you about my sailing days?' John asked a crowd of boys who were cursing and swearing at each other. It looked as though there was going to be a fight.

'You're a minister not a sailor,' one of them said cheekily.

'But I used to be a sailor. In fact, I was a ship's captain.'

'You were what!' several said together.

'Let me sit down, and I'll tell you about it.'

John perched himself on a wall and the boys stood round about him.

'I was a full-time working sailor from the day I was eleven,' he told them. 'And I've had some adventures in my time.'

'Tell us one,' the tallest boy said, not quite believing if what John was saying was true.

'One night, when I was sound asleep, there was a great crash above me. I was up on deck before I was properly awake. It was just chaos!'

'What had happened?' a little lad asked.

'I'll tell you what happened. One of the masts had broken in two and had crashed down on to the deck.'

'Was anyone killed,' someone asked gleefully.

'No,' John explained. 'Nobody was killed, but a man had been knocked overboard.'

'Into the water?'

'That's right! He was caught by the sail when the mast fell and trailed over the edge into the water.'

'I wouldn't like that,' announced a cheeky-faced boy. 'I don't like water.'

When the minister looked at the ingrained dirt on every part of the child's body and clothes, he totally believed what was told him.

'What happened next?' the lad demanded.

'The Captain called for ropes and threw them down to the man who was in danger of being dashed against the ship because it was so stormy. Then one of the crew tied a rope round his waist and lowered himself over the side. You see, the sea was thrusting the drowning man in the direction of the ship rather than away from it. The crewman grabbed the poor sailor's arm and held him tight. Next the Mate roped himself up and went over the side to help. Between the pair of them they managed to haul the man back to safety.'

'That was exciting!' the oldest boy said.

John laughed. 'I don't think it was in the least bit exciting for the men in the water.'

'Will you tell us a story?' the boys asked, every time they met John in the street, and when he had time he sat on a wall and did just that.

'Would you like to make some model boats?' he asked them, when he felt he knew them quite well.

'Yes,' they all yelled at once.

'Then tomorrow afternoon you come to my home and we'll begin whittling down some model boats.'

The following day he had a woodwork class!

'Is Mr. Newton in?' very dirty little boys who often came to the door asked the maid. At first she was not at all sure about this. But John told her that unless he was in his study working she should always let him know when his young friends called.

'Friends!' the maid thought, as she went into the kitchen. 'Mr. Newton has very strange taste in friends.'

'Would you like me to tell you another sea story?' he asked the boys one day when they all seemed to be there. He didn't need to wait for an answer.

'One day, a man called Jesus was in a boat with his friends. It was a nice day when they set out and, because Jesus was very tired, he fell sound asleep. His friends had been fishermen so they knew all about boats. But suddenly a terrible storm blew up. It was so bad that even the fishermen were frightened. They thought they were going to drown. One of them wakened Jesus. He stood up in the middle of the boat and commanded the wind to stop blowing and the sea to be still. Immediately it was calm! The wind and the sea did just what Jesus told them. And I'll tell you why they did. Jesus is the Son of God. He made the wind and the sea and they still do what he tells them.'

'That's the best story you've told us yet,' the cheeky-faced boy announced.

'Would you like to hear more like it?' John asked.

All the boys said they would.

'I tell you what,' the minister said. 'I'll start a weekly children's meeting and you can come along to that. And every single week I'll tell you another story about Jesus. How does that sound?'

'That sounds great,' the boys agreed.

When his young visitors had disappeared into the street again, John wrote to a friend of his in London.

'I have about twenty little lambs,' he wrote, 'each one of them worth more that all the animals that would sell in a market in seven years! Now I need your help. Could you please send me books I can use to teach them about the Lord.'

John's work with children was not always easy because some of those who came were real ruffians. From time to time they had him nearly tearing his hair out. But they continued coming, sometimes as many as two hundred at a time! A very wealthy man heard about the crowd and let John use a big empty house he owned in Olney for children's meetings and other meetings too. John had no children of his own, but plenty belonging to other people saw him as their friend.

The Collapse of a Camel

'I'll have to go home to look after my father,' Mary told her husband, when she heard how ill the old man was. 'And I may be able to help care for little Betsy while I'm there.'

John looked gloomy.

'While I know you should go, I can't bear to be without you again,' he sighed. 'Some people's love seems to grow cold as the years pass, but we've been married 26 years now, and I love you more every year and miss you more every time you're away.'

'But he needs me,' Mary insisted.

John pulled himself together. He stopped moaning and started planning. Very soon the arrangements for the journey were made. But Betsy was a bigger problem.

'It's no life for a five-year-old being brought up by maids and only seeing her father for a short time each day, if that,' Mary thought aloud.

'Your brother has done well,' her husband pointed out. 'It's five years since Betsy was born and his young wife died. But I wonder if he can go on like this. I don't know if it's fair to the child.'

But when Mary arrived at her father's home she

discovered that her brother was not really coping very well at all. The Newtons became even more concerned about their little niece. Then just a few months later, Mary's brother took ill and died. Betsy was an orphan.

'What can we do for the poor child?' Mary asked, when she heard the news.

'We can adopt Betsy and bring her up as our own,' said John immediately.

Betsy's grandfather wasn't too sure about this arrangement. He didn't think that middle-aged parents and life in a minister's home were quite right for a lively young girl.

'Have you ever heard them laugh so much?' the maid asked the woman who cooked for the Newtons. 'Since that little lady came this place is just full of laughter.'

'Apart from when Betsy's being naughty,' pointed out the cook. 'I'm glad to see that Mr. Newton takes a firm line when it comes to discipline.'

The maid agreed. 'He would have to. She's been so used to getting her own way that she thinks that everyone should dance attention on her.'

'Poor little mite. What sadness she's had in her life,' the cook said, shaking her head at the thought.

'That's as may be,' commented the maid, 'but she'll have a happier life with Mr. and Mrs. Newton than many children in Olney. They just love the child.'

As she finished her sentence, there was a crash in the

hall outside the kitchen followed by howls of laughter.

'What do you think Mr. Newton is up to now?' the cook asked.

There was a knock at the kitchen door, and the shamefaced minister explained himself. 'I'm sorry if we disturbed you, but it is rather difficult being a camel and carrying both a passenger and a load of brass plate for sale at the bazaar. Thankfully the passenger, Miss Betsy, stayed securely on my back but the brass plate was more difficult to manage.'

He closed the door behind him and gathered up what had fallen. Betsy was nowhere to be seen, she was off on another adventure.

'Camel!' laughed the cook. 'Mr. Newton a camel!'

The maid could hardly speak for giggling. 'A bazaar in the kitchen corridor! What next?'

When Mary's father eventually went to live with John and Mary it didn't take him long to discover that he'd been wrong. Betsy was having a wonderful life with her new middle-aged parents, and that particular minister's house was a lively and happy place for her to call home.

For two years the walls rang with Betsy's laughter and John was often the cause of it. Mary, however, never had good health and sometimes the little girl completely tired her out. When that happened John took Betsy into his study and entertained her with seafaring stories, each one more interesting than the one that went before.

'Tell me a story,' she pleaded, several times most days.

If John had time he sat with her on his knee and did just that, but one story he always made time for was her daily Bible story. And that, for him, was an almost perfect part of each day. Mary loved to see them together at Bible story time. Apart from anything else, it kept Betsy quiet!

'Today's story is a very interesting one,' John told Betsy after she'd had her tea one day. Betsy settled quietly on his knee and waited. 'Jesus had three friends, a man called Lazarus and his two sisters, Martha and Mary. When Jesus was some distance away the brother took ill and died. His sisters were very upset, especially because they thought that if Jesus had been there Lazarus might not have died at all.'

Betsy was riveted. She knew a lot about people dying.

'After a few days Jesus went to visit the sisters. One of them actually told him that if he had been there his friend would not have died. Jesus was very sad because he loved his friends very much.'

'What happened next, Nuncle?' the child asked.

John smiled. He loved when she used his pet name.

'Jesus went to where Lazarus was buried, and shouted for him to come out of the tomb. And an amazing thing happened. The dead man was made alive again, just at the sound of Jesus' voice, and he walked out of the tomb to Jesus.'

The little girl's eyes were round like saucers.

'Could Jesus make me alive again after I die?' she asked.

'Yes, Betsy, Jesus can do that. If you put your trust in the Lord Jesus, when you die Jesus will take you to live for ever and ever with him in heaven.'

She hugged him close.

'I don't want to die,' she said. 'Father and Mother died, but I don't want to die, not ever.'

'We all have to die unless Jesus comes back first,' John said soothingly.

'Even little girls?'

'Yes, my dear, even little girls die. That's why it's so important that you trust in the Lord Jesus.'

Betsy nodded. 'But I still don't want to die until I'm very, very old.'

John hugged Betsy goodnight with a heavier heart than usual. He sighed. So many children died in England, so many families lost little ones.*

'It's very exciting!' Betsy laughed, just after her seventh birthday. 'I'm going to school!'

The maid tried not to look upset. 'Imagine you being old enough to go to boarding school' she said. 'But Mr. Newton sometimes teaches there so you'll see him often.'

'I know that, and I'm already looking forward to

* At that time in England one child out of every four died.

his visits. Do you think Nuncle will bring me little gifts when he comes?'

The maid thought of all the little things John had brought home for Betsy and assured her that he would likely do that.

When Betsy left for school there was a silence about the house that seemed thick enough to cut with a knife.

'I don't miss the noise,' Mary said, 'but I miss Betsy such a lot. I'll write to her today in case she's missing us.'

John looked up from his book. 'She'll have so much going on around her I'm sure she'll be happy as can be. It is just we who are silent and miserable.'

'That's not quite true,' a voice said behind him. He hadn't realised the maid was in the room. 'Cook and I hardly know what to say to each other. For the last two years most of our talk has been about Miss Betsy.'

'Are you writing to the dear girl?' Mary asked later that evening, when John settled down at his desk.

'No,' he said. 'I'm working on a hymn.'

'I've never met anyone like you,' his wife smiled. 'If you can't find a hymn that says exactly what you want it to say, you just sit down and write one!'

'You make it sound easy, but it can be hard work sometimes.'

Mary sat back in her chair beside the fireplace. 'Will you sing me my favourite one of your hymns?' she asked.

John didn't need to ask which that was.

Starting in a quiet voice, that grew louder with each verse, he sang the hymn that his wife most wanted.

Amazing grace! How sweet the sound,
That saved a wretch like me!
I once was lost, but now I'm found,
Was blind, but now I see.

John thought of the day he nearly died at sea.

'Twas grace that taught my heart to fear,
And grace my fears relieved;
How precious did that grace appear
The hour I first believed!

Through many dangers, toils and snares
I have already come;
'Tis grace has brought me safe this far,
And grace will lead me home.'

Mary joined in when John reached the last verse, a verse that spoke of heaven.

'When I've been there a thousand years,
Bright shining as the sun
I've no less days to sing God's praise
Than when I first begun.'

* * *

Although there was peace and quiet inside the Olney minister's house after Betsy went to school, there was plenty of noise outside. Things were hard in the lace-making industry and many people were going hungry.

'There's been a flour raid,' John told his wife one cold afternoon. 'These poor men are desperate to find food for their families. They saw the flour being driven from the market and took their chance.'

Mary sighed. 'We do all we can to help them,' she said, thinking of the bundles of food she had given her maid to deliver to the poorest of the homes.

'And those sad people whose homes were destroyed in the fire, they're not only hungry but homeless as well.'

'The relief fund you set up is bringing in money to help them,' Mary reminded him.

'But it is only a drop in the ocean,' he said sadly. 'There is so much need and so little being done. Unless things get better soon the situation in the town could become ugly.'

John was quite right. Things did get ugly, and he wrote to tell a friend just how bad it was.

'A wild and lawless mob paraded the streets, breaking windows and extorting money from one end of the town to the other. My house was expressly threatened. I believe if I had gone out to speak with them I might have had so much influence as to have saved my windows. The worst of those in the mob, taken singly and sober, seem to have some respect for me, but together and drunk they are terrible creatures. About 10 pm, 40 or 50 of them came to attack the house. My wife was so terrified that I was forced to send out a gentle message to them and to give a shilling to the leader of the mob to secure his protection. I'm ashamed that I couldn't do better than that.'

Changes were happening in Olney, and it was time for a change for the Newtons. Toward the end of 1779, John and Mary moved from Olney to St. Mary Woolnoth in London. John wrote to tell Betsy what their new home was like.

'There are green trees in front, and a green field behind with cows feeding in it; so it has some little resemblance of the country.'

Betsy could hardly wait for her first holiday. The idea of having a field of cows just outside of her window appealed to her greatly.

Satan, Self and Company

John was pacing up and down his study when his wife knocked on the door.

'Is there something worrying you?' she asked. 'You've been walking backwards and forwards so long that I've come to see if you've worn out the rug.'

Newton plumped himself down on his chair.

'There are disadvantages in being a minister in the city of London,' he said. 'One is the noise and another is the pomp and ceremony.'

Mary nodded. She had known all along what was worrying her husband.

'I'm quite happy for the Lord Mayor to come to our church for his annual visit. And I'm delighted that the custom is to have a visiting preacher for the occasion. But what I don't like is the thought of a grand dinner at the Mansion House afterwards. That's not the proper way to spend a Sunday.'

'I hear what you're saying,' his wife said. 'But don't you think you'd better go as this is the first time the Lord Mayor has been here since we came to London.'

John didn't hear her, so absorbed was he in thinking of some excuse to get out of the Mansion House dinner.

The day of the Lord Mayor's visit dawned bright, and John had a smile on his face.

'I quite understand that you're not able to attend the dinner,' the Lord Mayor said sympathetically. 'You would have a problem eating the meal with your arm in a sling. It was very good of you to come to the service at all after your accident.'

'Leading the congregation in prayer wasn't a problem,' John said. 'But eating is rather difficult.'

Later, as the Lord Mayor and his entourage left the church for the Mansion House, John walked home smiling.

'Are you sure you didn't fall deliberately?' Mary teased, as she cut up the meat on his plate to make it easier to eat with only a fork.

Her husband laughed. 'All I did was put my foot carelessly on that stone just outside the front door. It didn't occur to me that it would move, and that I'd be thrown over a post and dislocate my shoulder!' There was a pause. 'But I can't say I'm terribly sorry it happened!'

Less than a year after moving to London, the Newtons were plunged into sadness.

'It's such a tragedy,' Mary said. 'Nearly the whole family wiped out, and so suddenly.'

John said nothing, thinking it was good to let his wife talk through her grief at what had happened to her sister, Elizabeth, and her family.

'First little Jackie and Susie died. And when Elizabeth

was caring for them, her husband suddenly died. Now Elizabeth is so ill herself that she can't look after Eliza. Poor child, she must be brokenhearted to lose her brother, sister and father in such a short space of time.'

'I think you should write offering Elizabeth and Eliza a home with us,' John said.

Mary nodded. 'Yes,' she said. 'I think we should do that.'

But by the time the letter arrived, Elizabeth was so poorly that only Eliza was able to make the journey to her uncle and aunt's home in London.

'The child is so ill,' John worried aloud, soon after fourteen-year-old Eliza arrived. 'She has consumption like her mother.'

His wife nodded. 'Eliza knows her mother is dying and she wants to die too.'

Thinking of the conversation he had had with the girl the previous night, John knew what his wife was saying was true.

'But we must do what we can to help her get better. It may be that God has work for her to do yet.'

'And pray that Betsy doesn't catch it from her cousin,' Mary said anxiously. 'It's lovely for the girls to have each other, but dangerous for Betsy.'

As she spoke there was a rush at the door.

'Uncle-puncle,' Betsy laughed, 'You've not told Eliza any of your sea stories yet.'

Eliza came in more slowly, coughing into a handkerchief as she came.

'Well,' John said, 'this is as good a time as any. If you sit still for a story, Eliza, your coughing might ease.'

The two girls sat together to listen, and Mary was glad to see that Eliza covered her mouth with her hankie each time she coughed. Consumption was a terrible disease and so easily spread from one to another.

'Is Eliza going to die?' Betsy asked John some weeks later. Her cousin was having to spend more and more of each day resting.

John looked at the twelve-year-old's serious face.

'We're doing everything we can for her,' he said softly, 'but she doesn't seem to be improving.'

'If Eliza dies I want to die too,' sobbed the girl. 'Life's horrible! I just want to die!'

John sat down heavily. With his arm round Betsy, he spoke to her about death and dying. Then he talked about heaven and Jesus' promise to prepare a place for his people there so that they could spend forever in his company.

'There's a sense in which it's not wrong to want to die,' John said, 'because heaven will be so much better than earth. But it's not right to want to die just to escape from horrible things.'

'But I do want to die,' Betsy cried. 'I want to get away from all this sadness and sickness and be with Jesus.'

John looked at the girl. It hurt him to see her so distressed.

'I understand,' he said. 'But you're forgetting

something. Jesus said his people would be with him forever in heaven, but he also said that he would be with his people on earth.'

Betsy nodded. 'I know he said that, but it doesn't feel as though he's with us just now.'

And with all the terrible grief of a twelve-year-old, the girl wept until she had no more tears. But there were more tears to come. Before many weeks had passed Eliza died and Betsy lost her cousin and friend.

'I am going to the vestry,' John told his wife one afternoon. 'I'll be back in time for tea … I hope.'

Mary laughed. 'I hope so too. Yesterday you were so late that the warm buttered crumpets, that were meant to be a treat for you, were cold and stuck to the plate!'

'I can't help it if people find that it is the best place to talk to me about their problems,' John said. 'I'm just grateful they do, though I don't always feel I'm able to help them.'

The minister was no sooner installed in his vestry than there was a knock at the door. In response to his request to come in, a middle-aged woman bustled into the room.

'Mrs. Smith,' John said, rising to his feet. 'It's good to see you. Please take a seat.'

The woman sat down and a few minutes were spent in polite conversation. But Mrs. Smith was so agitated that John came right to the point.

'As you've come here to see me, I assume you have something you want to say.'

The woman's face broke into a wide smile.

'Mr. Newton,' she began, 'I came to tell you some wonderful news so that you might rejoice with me.'

John relaxed. He'd had a trying morning, and some good news was just what he needed.

'Indeed,' he smiled. 'And what is your good news?'

Very pleased with herself, the woman could hardly speak for excitement.

'It's like this,' she said. 'I bought a lottery ticket and … and …'

John's smile melted. 'And?' he enquired.

Words came tumbling out. '… and I've won a substantial amount of money! I'm so thrilled and I just couldn't wait to come to tell you so that you could rejoice with me in my good fortune and say a prayer of thanks for the money.'

Having finished her excited story, the woman sat back in her chair and beamed … until she noticed the change in her minister's expression.

'Madam,' he said solemnly, 'as you are a friend undergoing temptation I will pray for you.'

Without waiting for a response, he bowed his head and prayed that she would never again be tempted to gamble on a lottery, and that she would be content with what God had given her rather than try to win something for nothing. After John finished praying there was an uncomfortable silence. Then Mrs. Smith rose to her feet, thanked him, and left with tears in her eyes.

John Newton was grateful for the half-hour break before the next person knocked on his door. And when the door did open again the caller could not have been more different from Mrs. Smith. The minister very soon realised he was dealing with a troubled man. He listened carefully to what he was told.

'I really need your advice,' the visitor said. 'You see, I have been under such attack. When I try to read my Bible my thoughts wander all over the place. And when I try to pray my mind thinks about everything but prayer. Even in church I can't concentrate. I feel as though Satan wins every single battle.'

'You sound very tired,' John said perceptively. 'Is there a reason for that?'

Mr. Black nodded. 'I'm not sleeping well. My mind just won't turn off. And if I do sleep I have such disturbing dreams that I'd rather be awake.'

John looked at the poor man. He knew him well and knew that his work was very demanding, and that there were pressures at home too.

'Do you think I've lost my faith?' Mr. Black asked, his voice wavering.

John shook his head.

'No,' he said. 'I don't think that. And if that's what it feels like, remember that your faith is based on God's faithfulness not yours. He'll not let you down.'

Mr. Black sighed with relief. It was as though a

weight had been taken off his shoulders.

'And I think what you are needing more than anything else is a holiday by the sea.'

'A holiday?' the man said, very surprised at the suggestion. 'I thought you'd preach a sermon at me, and instead you tell me to take a holiday!'

The minister smiled. 'You have two sermons each Sunday,' he said. 'But what you need is a holiday from the stresses you're living under. It's because you're so tired that you don't have the energy to fight temptation. A holiday will make a big difference.'

When Mr. Black knocked on the vestry door he had been a very worried man, but when he left he was already feeling much better.

The door had hardly closed when there was another knock and several men walked it.

John's eyebrows rose. He knew the men. They were City bankers and among the wealthiest men in his congregation, though not among the most faithful.

'How can I help you, gentlemen?' he asked.

The men had obviously already decided who would be their spokesman. All remained silent apart from a tall, dark-haired man who immediately launched into a story about troubles in the world of high finance, about interest rates falling and investments doing badly. John listened. Each one of these men was well-off. None of them knew what it was like to be cold or hungry. They had maids to look after their every need, nannies for their children, holidays when and where they wanted.

Not only that, they had money left over to invest. John shook himself and tried to concentrate on what he was being told. The dark-haired man was still speaking, still moaning and complaining. Eventually Newton raised his hand to indicate that he'd heard enough.

'There is a great and old established firm,' he told the men. 'And it does a lot of business. Unfortunately it also does a lot of harm, both in the world of finance and in the church.'

The men looked interested.

'And the name of this firm?' John went on. 'The name of this firm is Satan, Self and Company.'

There was an uncomfortable shuffling in the room and none of the men would meet his eye.

'It seems to me from what I have heard that you may be working for Satan, Self and Company,' the minister continued. 'And if you are, I earnestly suggest that you change your employer.'

Within a very short time the men made their excuses and left the vestry.

'Satan, Self and Company!' one of them spat, as the door closed behind them. 'How dare he say that to us!'

But two of the others looked at each other with a different expression. They wondered if John Newton might just be right after all.

'Am I on time for crumpets?' John asked, when he arrived home.

Mary came to meet him. 'You are indeed,' she said.

'You must have had a dull time in the vestry today for you to be home so early.'

John kept the vestry secrets to himself, but he smiled as he ate his crumpets. 'A dull time?' he wondered. 'I don't think so!'

Enter William Wilberforce

One Sunday in December 1785 there was a knock on the door of John's vestry.

'Come in,' he called.

A young man entered and handed the minister a letter. When John opened it, the first thing he noticed was the sweeping signature at the bottom. Then he read what was written and looked up at the young man.

'Your postscript is rather dramatic,' John said, reading what was written at the bottom of the letter. 'Remember that I must be secret, and that the gallery of the House is now so universally attended, because the face of a Member of Parliament is pretty well known.'

The young man looked serious.

'You are indeed well-known, Mr. William Wilberforce,' John said. 'And you're not the first member of the Wilberforce family I've had the privilege of meeting. I count some of your uncles among my best friends.'

William began to relax.

'Your secret coming is safe with me, but I think you have other secrets you wish to share.'

The young man sat with his hands clasped tight.

'Please tell me what you know about me,' he asked.

John thought for a moment before answering.

'I know you are a Member of Parliament and close friends with our new Prime Minister, William Pitt. I know that in your earlier days a Christian aunt tried to influence you regarding belief in Jesus Christ. But I know also that your parents at that stage of your upbringing preferred that you spend your time doing other things. And lastly, I know that you studied at Cambridge before taking a seat in Parliament, where you began to make your mark right away.'

William looked the minister in the eye. 'You choose your words carefully,' he said. 'You've told me what you know, but there are other things you have heard. Are there not?'

'Indeed there are,' John said. 'But I do not know them to be true.'

'Then let me confess that they probably are. I am a member of five exclusive clubs. In any one of them I think little of gambling away a hundred pounds a night, or winning a hundred or two. I have friends in high society and some who befriend me for what they think they'll get out of it. And if my acquaintances were to discover that I frequented a vestry, they would think me mad. Perhaps I am. But mad or not, I would like to speak with you.'

An arrangement was made that the young man would visit John in his home.

* * *

'A gentleman is at the door to see you,' Newton's maid announced. 'But he will not give his name.'

'Show him in,' John said. 'I know who he is.'

William came in and sat down. There was a minute of silence, but not an awkward one.

'I walked round the square several times before plucking up courage to come to the door,' William said.

John smiled. 'I know. I saw you.'

William sat back in his chair. 'I see there is no point in dodging issues with you,' he laughed, 'so I might as well pour it all out.'

His host nodded in agreement.

'I live a busy life,' Wilberforce said. 'I work hard in Parliament, and I play hard when I'm not working. My free time is jam-packed full of parties, dances, clubs and the theatre. There is hardly a free hour in my diary. But I don't need as much as a whole hour free to be uncomfortable with what my mind and conscience trawl up when they are not otherwise employed. You see, for all that I have and all that I do, I know there is something missing in my life. I fill my days and I fill my nights too, but there is still something missing.'

'And what makes you think I can help you find what's missing?' John asked.

'I was travelling in Europe with a friend, Isaac Milner. You know him; he visited you at Olney.'

John nodded.

'Yes,' he said. 'I remember Isaac well.'

William Wilberforce continued.

'We had some discussions that encouraged me to read the New Testament, and when I'd read it I knew I had to live a very different sort of life. So I tried and tried .....'

As the minister listened to the young man's story it was as though he was reliving his own life. William had gone though the same struggles as he had in his youth: trying to live a decent life and always failing, sometimes immediately and other times being able to keep it up a little longer. But sooner or later always ending in failure.

'What should I do?' William asked. 'Should I renounce my wealth, give up politics? Should I stop being part of high society, or maybe become a minister of religion?'

And having said all he had to say, the young man slumped back in his chair exhausted.

As he walked home, William thought over the advice John had given him.

'Mr. Newton said not to give up politics.' He scratched his head in bewilderment. 'Then he told me not to cut myself off from society or give away all I own. But the hardest bit of advice he gave was that I should talk this over with the Prime Minister. William Pitt's a good friend, and I don't want him to think I've become a religious freak.'

Hard though it was, William tried to follow the

older man's advice. And as visit followed visit, the two of them became good friends. Not only that, William Wilberforce became a Christian, a son of God, which made them brothers as well as friends.

'There is something I want to talk about,' William said, as they enjoyed an afternoon together.

'What's that?' asked John.

'At the risk of bringing back unpleasant memories, I want to talk about the slave trade.'

John was not surprised as he knew his young friend had a longing to do good to those who most needed it.

William said what was on his mind. 'A few years ago Lord North said that the slave trade was an economic necessity. He argued that plantations producing cotton, sugar and rum could not survive without slave labour. Furthermore, he said that if the slave trade stopped, the bottom would go out of the shipbuilding industry. Many ships are built just to transport slaves from Africa to the Americas. Not only that, Lord North declared that if slavery was abolished and the slave ships no longer sailed, there would not be enough trained sailors to serve in the Royal Navy.'

'He made quite an impression,' John said.

But William wasn't finished. 'The argument which really sickened me was the one that suggested that slavery had a civilizing effect on the people who were torn from their families and communities and taken to the other side of the world to be worked to death!

How could they say that?'

John sighed, and tried to explain.

'I think the idea is that they would never hear about the Lord in their African villages, where they might as they voyaged if the sailors were Christians. And they might when they arrived if their owners were Christians.'

The young man raised his eyebrows.

'You mean they might believe in a God of love because people chained them together in the hold of a ship or whipped them for not working hard enough in a sugar plantation?'

John's sad eyes reflected his change of thinking on the subject of slavery, a change that had taken place over many years.

'My old business is one that makes my heart shudder,' he said quietly. 'There were some good people in the slave trade,' John continued, 'but mostly bad. And I'll tell you a story to show you how bad it could be. The Mate on one ship bought a woman who had a healthy child about a year old. In the night the child cried a lot and disturbed the Mate's sleep. He got into such a bad temper that he told the woman that if she didn't silence the child, he would. But the little one went on crying. Eventually he tore the child from its mother's arms and threw it into the sea. Although the mother wanted to go after the child, to save it or to die, he held her on board the ship. She was worth too much money to him.'

William's heart went out to his old friend as he relived that awful memory. But, although he didn't want to upset John, he knew that the subject had to be tackled, and that Newton was the one to help him.

John went on, 'I have seen people whipped unmercifully until they hadn't even the strength to groan when the whip hit them. I've seen slaves in thumbscrews for days at a time, with the screws being tightened torturously.'

'You're in a unique position,' William told John, after a long discussion on the subject. 'You've seen the slave trade at first hand and you've thought through the subject in the years since then. Although I'm doing my best to have it abolished, all I know is second-hand.'

John looked at the young man.

'What are you thinking?' asked William.

'I'm thinking that you are the answer to my prayers. When I was a trader I really didn't see the awfulness of what I was doing. Honestly. Even after I became a Christian I didn't realise the horror of the work I was involved in. Mary did. She hated what I did and was never happier than when I took a fit, the only one I ever had, the day before I was to set sail in a brand new slave ship. Looking back, I wonder at how blind I was.'

In the pause that followed a pained look crossed John's face.

'Please don't think though that I ever considered slaves as less than human. I didn't, though there were many who did, who thought they didn't feel things in the same way we did. They thought these poor people fitted in somewhere between animals and human beings.'

'You said I might be the answer to your prayers,' his young friend reminded him. 'In what way?'

Newton nodded. 'I've been praying for a long time now that brave men would take up the cause to abolish the slave trade. And I think that you will be their leader.'

William looked the old man in the eye. 'Then keep praying,' he said. 'Keep praying.'

John thought about that conversation long after William had left for home. The thought that kept coming into his mind over the following days and weeks was that he could write a booklet about the slave trade, a first-hand account, perhaps even including a confession of his own involvement. Taking up his pen, he wrote 'Thoughts upon the African Slave Trade.' And as the ink dried he knew for sure that this was a job he had to do.

'How does this sound?' John asked William, when he came to visit one day. John read some paragraphs from the beginning of the manuscript.

'Read the second paragraph again, please,' the young man asked.

Newton cleared his throat. 'If I attempt to throw my little bit into the public stock of information on slavery, it is not mainly because I think that my contribution is necessary, it is more from a conviction that silence, at such a time as this, would be criminal … I am bound in conscience to take shame on myself by a public confession, which, however sincere, comes too late to prevent or repair the misery and trouble of which I was once a part.'

'You're a brave man,' William said.

John shook his head. 'No, I'm an old man. I'm too old to campaign as you are doing. In any case, God has given me other work to do. But what I can do is be honest about what I know to be true. It is for you and other brave young men to take up the cause and to fight to the very end.

William Wilberforce attended John Newton's church. Sunday after Sunday as he left the service, he would tell his old friend how the campaign was going. And as often as he could he visited the Newtons' home. On one of these visits, William had news for John.

'Your booklet has really stirred up public opinion. People are grouping together and forming local associations to campaign for the abolition of slavery. It's becoming a big issue, John. It's what everyone is talking about.'

Victory at Long Last!

Having opened his diary at May 1789, John Newton took up his pen and began to write.

'Today William addressed the House of Commons for three-and-a-half hours. I heard his speech described as impressive and eloquent. It would be all that. Young though he is, William Wilberforce will raise support to abolish the slave trade if anyone can. But I must keep praying for him.'

The following day, when he read over what he had written, John added a little bit to it.

'I must impress on William that there is work to be done even after trading in slavery is a thing of the past. The next big job will be to free those who are already slaves, and there are thousands of them. There will be terrific opposition from their owners because they'll have to employ people to do the work the slaves are doing just now, and they'll have to pay them as well.'

John laid down his pen, sat back in his chair, and thought through the subject. Slave trading had been carried on since 1713, he remembered, and it was estimated that the number of slaves taken from their families and transported across the Atlantic Ocean was more than 100,000, half of them in British ships.

The old man shook his head at the thought. '100,000,' he repeated to himself, 'of which maybe as many as 30,000 died before ever reaching dry land. And I heard it said that the average lifespan of a slave working the plantations is just seven years. What a waste of life! '

'Mr. Wilberforce is here,' John's maid told him. Although it was springtime Newton had a rug round him to keep him warm. The older he became, the more he felt the cold.

'Dear boy!' John said in welcome.

'Dear old Newton! Your friend is no longer a boy. I'm thirty today!'

'Well, well,' the minister laughed. 'You think you're no longer a boy at thirty! Just wait till you're my age and you'll realise just how young that is!'

'How old are you?' William asked.

'Too old to keep count of it! But Betsy does, and she tells me I'm 64, though I can't quite believe it!'

A thought crossed John's mind.

'I was almost exactly your age, William, when I had that seizure and *The Bee* sailed without me. I was just coming up to my thirtieth birthday when I left the slave trade behind me.'

Wilberforce's face suddenly became serious. 'There is something we've got to talk about,' he said, 'and it's urgent.'

John indicated to his friend to go on.

'We're getting a lot of support for the abolition

of slavery in the Americas and West Indies. A growing number of people are right behind us. Some of them even want to boycott goods produced in plantations worked by slaves. They're asking their friends not to buy sugar, cotton and rum as a protest.'

'I've heard that,' John said. 'But I'm not sure it's a good idea. It will annoy more people than it will help.'

'That's exactly what I've told them,' William said. 'But that's not what we must discuss.'

'What's the problem, dear boy?' John asked.

Wilberforce sighed. 'The problem is this. It's all very well campaigning for the abolition of the slave trade, but we've also got to think about freeing those who are already slaves.'

John nodded. 'I've not forgotten them,' he agreed. 'But that will be a big job. There are tens of thousands of slaves on the other side of the Atlantic.'

William slapped his thigh. 'So there are, but there are also about 14,000 slaves here in Britain. It's the in-thing to have an African slave in better-off households. It would make good sense to begin by freeing those on our doorstep before doing anything elsewhere.'

John agreed, and they discussed what might be done for them.

With all the energy of a young enthusiast, Wilberforce worked to get a bill to abolish the British slave trade through the Houses of Parliament. Slowly and surely attitudes changed. One such change was a real encouragement to John Newton, whose concern for freeing those who were in slavery never left him.

'I have news for you today,' William said, as he walked into John's study unannounced.

The older man closed the book he was reading.

'Then you'd better sit down and tell me what it is.'

He could see that William was excited, so he teased him a little.

'I was preparing my sermon for Sunday. But I suppose the congregation will understand if I tell them I didn't get it finished because a friend of mine had news for me.'

Wilberforce laughed. 'Will you be quiet and listen,' he said.

Newton sat back in his chair and waited.

'I've just heard that the new Colony of Sierra Leone has been officially established. Free slaves now have a homeland of their own in West Africa. The capital is to be called Freetown and freed slaves from Britain will be among its first citizens. It's hoped that before long they'll be joined by others from the Americas.'

'That is good news indeed,' John exclaimed. 'May God bless Sierra Leone and all those who'll live there!'

Both men fell silent. It was William who spoke first.

'I've been thinking,' he said. 'Many British slaves were born into slavery, and most of their parents too. Freedom is not going to be easy for them. They've never had to make decisions, let alone decisions about government or national finance. We're asking them to do important jobs for which they have neither training nor experience. I fear that Sierra Leone will be a troubled land before it's a peaceful one.'

'I'm sure it will,' John agreed sadly. 'You can set slaves free but you can't undo what slavery has done to them. It will take generations before the children of freed slaves are truly free in their minds as well as their bodies.'

'But we've got to keep trying,' said William. 'The sooner the trade is abolished the sooner that day of true freedom will come.'

After his visitor had left, John turned the globe of the world until America was facing him. He traced a line from Carolina to the West Indies, then from the West Indies across the South Atlantic to West Africa. He remembered his voyages going in the opposite direction, on ships with their holds full of men, women and children that had been captured them from their villages. He could almost smell the stench from the hold, and hear the cries of children sold separately from their parents. John sat down heavily.

'What will their journey back be like when they are freed?' he wondered. 'They'll be passengers then, not cargo.'

He sat in silence for a long time, his mind reliving incident after awful incident.

'How I wish I could undo what I did all these years ago,' he thought.

The door opened and Betsy bustled in to put coal

on the dying embers of the fire.

'Sorry,' she said, seeing John jump. 'You were miles away!'

John smiled. 'I certainly was,' he agreed. 'But I'm back now and tea and hot toast would be a good welcome home.'

'I thought I'd join you for tea,' Mary said, coming behind Betsy.

The smell of buttered toast rose from the tray Mary was carrying.

John rose and helped her to a chair. He looked at his wife as they drank their tea. She was so frail. They had known for over a year that she had cancer and would not get better. But over the last few weeks she seemed to have gone downhill very quickly.

'Are you comfortable?' he asked gently.

'The pain is not so bad today,' Mary said. But something in her eyes made him anxious. There was a look of fear in them that John had never seen before.

'I don't want to die,' she said suddenly. 'I'm scared to die. I'm so scared.'

John put his arms round his wife, but she pushed him away.

'You wouldn't want to do that if you really knew me,' she cried. 'You think I'm a Christian and I'm not. And I'll go to hell when I die ... I'm so very scared.'

Mary pulled her apron up over her face and wept like a brokenhearted child. Hearing the noise, Betsy rushed into the room and did what she could to help.

For two long and terrible weeks Mary Newton was tortured with thoughts of dying and going to hell.

'Dearest Mary,' John told her, over and over and over again, 'God is holding you in the hollow of his hand, and you're absolutely safe there even though you don't feel it.'

His wife shook her head. She hardly spoke at all some days. John spent hours with her, telling her that Jesus loved her and had died for her. He reminded her that Jesus always keeps his promises, and that he has promised that all his children will go to heaven to be with him. When John saw his wife becoming more and more ill, he prayed that she would regain her peace of mind before she died. God heard his prayer and Mary's mind settled and she was calm again. For the next three months, until December 1790, the Newtons were able to talk about the future, realising that Mary's future would soon be in heaven. Ten days before Christmas, John sat beside the bed of his dying wife. The candle he held threw his shadow grotesquely on to the wall behind the bed but nothing disturbed the peace of Mary's passing from earth to heaven. When she had gone, John picked up her Bible and read some verses his wife had underlined.

'Although the fig-tree shall not blossom, neither shall fruit be in the vines; the labour of the olive shall fail, and the fields shall yield no meat; the flock shall be cut off from the fold, and there shall be no herd in the stalls, yet I will rejoice in the Lord, I will joy in the

God of my salvation.'

John read the words over and over again. 'Yet I will rejoice in the Lord,' he said softly. 'Even though my dearest Mary has gone home to Jesus, even though I'll never see her again here on earth, yet I will rejoice in the Lord.'

Closing the Bible, he bowed his head in prayer before going to tell Betsy that her Mama was dead.

If John Newton had known that he would live for another 17 years after Mary's death he would have grieved terribly, for they had loved each other very much. But he did not know that. He lived the rest of his life one day at a time, knowing that each day was one day nearer heaven.

'1st January 1800,' John wrote, 'and the beginning of a new century. I can hardly believe that it's over ten years since Mary died. And what a lot has happened in that time. William Wilberforce continues to push for the abolition of slavery, but it's a long hard job. However, I'm convinced it will come before too long now. Each time parliament votes on it, the number that want to retain the trade diminishes. Perhaps next time the abolitionists will win the vote.'

John Newton's prayers were answered in 1804 when William's abolition motion was passed with a substantial majority. This meant that slave trading would soon be a thing of the past. By then John was 79 years old. It was half a century since he had worked in the slave trade, and now he was assured that no young Englishman would ever take that up as a career.

'It is a privilege to care for him,' Betsy told a friend who was visiting John Newton three years later. 'He has such sweetness of character and quietness of mind.'

The friend smiled. 'Do you know what he has just told me?'

Betsy asked what that might be.

'As I left he said that he was packed and sealed and waiting for the post. What a lovely way of thinking of death.'

'I can't imagine what life will be like without him,' said Betsy. 'He's been a wonderful father to me.'

On 21st December 1807, William Wilberforce called on John to tell him that another major step had been taken towards the freeing of slaves. And this was the last news that reached John Newton, because that was the day he died and went to meet his Lord Jesus. As Betsy looked at the old man for the last time she remembered back over the years to a day soon after she'd arrived in her uncle's home. He had pretended he was a camel and she was a grand lady perched on his back. They were going to the bazaar to sell some beautiful brass plates. On the way along the kitchen corridor the brass plates had crashed to the ground, giving the maid and cook a terrible fright. Although Betsy's heart was sore at her uncle's death, she smiled at the happy memory.

Thinking Further Topics

Chapter One

Meeting on Little Bear Quay

As a boy, John Newton felt different from other boys because his mother was always ill and his relationship with his father was strained. How do you cope with feeling different from other people, and how do you react when you meet people who are different from you?

John discovered some horrible things from the boys at Little Bear Quay. When he went home he discussed them with his mother. Are you able to talk things over with your parents? Young Christians, whose parents are not believers, often find it helpful to talk to an older Christian friend, someone at church or a Christian teacher at school.

Ephesians 6:1-4 has something to say about parents and children. Timothy was a young man whom the Apostle Paul befriended. Paul's letters to Timothy show the benefits of an older Christian encouraging a younger one. For example, 1 Timothy 4:7-8, 1 Timothy 6:11-12 and 2 Timothy 2:1.

Chapter Two

World's End and Beyond

John's mother died when he was just a little boy. Coping with the death of someone you love is never easy. It's hard to think that you'll never see someone again. It is different for Christians because they have God's promise that they will all go to heaven. But does that mean we should not feel sad when a Christian dies? How did Jesus feel when his friend Lazarus died? See John 11:32-36. Jesus remembers and understands what it is like to lose someone you love. The Bible says that as Christians we should not be sorrowful as though we have no hope when someone who loves Jesus has gone to be with him. We know for sure where they are - they are with the Lord, enjoying eternal life. That is a sure and certain hope for all who love the Lord Jesus Christ.

Newton married again after John's mother died. Is there anything wrong with doing that? Marriage is one of God's most precious gifts. Genesis 2:22-24 tells about God's creation of the very first marriage. John's life was difficult, but he still had things he enjoyed. One of his pleasures was spending time in the countryside. Genesis 1 describes the creation of all things. The study of God's creation will never disprove the existence of the Creator.

Chapter Three
Life on the Ocean Wave

There were no career choices for John Newton. His father made all the decisions. How do you cope when your parents seem to interfere with your choices? Do they sometimes know better than you do what's good for you? Nowadays young people choose their own careers, but should they seek their parents' advice? Jesus told a story about two boys: one followed his father's career choice for him and the other did absolutely his own thing. See Luke 15:11-32.

What things should you take into account when you are thinking about your career? Does Philippians 2:3-4 have anything to say on the subject?

John's mother had taught him about the Lord Jesus, but when he got into bad company he became as bad as the company he kept, sometimes worse. How does peer pressure affect you? Do you choose your friends carefully so that you are not influenced to do what's wrong?

Chapter Four

Help! We're sinking!

Many people cry out, 'God help me!' when they are in danger or trouble of some kind. Have we any right to ask God for help when we are in trouble if we ignore him when things are going well with us? How would you feel if someone was friends with you only when they wanted something from you?

John Newton's mother had taught him about the Lord Jesus. Over the years he had, from time to time, tried very hard to live a Christian life. But each time he ended up worse than he was when he started. What was different about John's experience in the shipwreck? Is there a difference between trying to live a good life and being a Christian?

What is a Christian? See John 3:16. Does that mean Christians only have to believe and it doesn't matter how they behave? James 2:20-23 has something to say about that idea.

Chapter Five

Human Cargo

Slavery was part of life in Jesus' day as it was when John Newton was alive. The short book of Philemon (it has only 25 verses) is the story of a slave who ran away from his Christian master. It's an interesting read. Not all slave owners were cruel, though as John Newton said, 'There was good and bad in the slave trade, mostly bad.'

It was Christians like Wilberforce who fought to have the slave trade abolished. Christians should always aim to change society for the better. What did Jesus mean in Matthew 5:13? Today Christians fight for social change through how they use their votes and by writing to Members of Parliament and others in authority. In what issues do you feel Christians should be campaigning for change? Paul gave Timothy some interesting advice about his relationship with governing authorities. See 1 Timothy 2:1-2.

Chapter Six

Aye, Aye, Captain Newton

It probably surprised you that when John Newton became a Christian he didn't give up the slave trade immediately. Do you take part in things without thinking if they are good or bad, just because they are what young folk do? Paul gave a very high set of ideals in Philippians 4:8-9. Could you use his advice to help you decide what you should take part in, what books and magazines you should read and what television programmes you should watch?

Some sailors thought John would be a soft mark because he was a Christian. Do you ever try to take advantage of people? If sailors did they were punished for it. John was a disciplinarian. If he had not been, his ship would have been chaotic. Do you think Christian parents should discipline their children? How should they do it? Should smacking be allowed? Solomon, who wrote the Book of Proverbs, was given a special gift of wisdom from God. What does Solomon say on the subject? See Proverbs 13:24.

Chapter Seven

Surveying the Tides

John only had one seizure in his life, on the day before he was due to leave on the slave ship, *The Bee*. Does God use circumstances to encourage us to do what he wants us to do? Or does God create the circumstances in the first place? Acts 27 – 28:16 tells a very exciting story about a storm and shipwreck, snake bites and danger. It's a splendid example of God's involvement in Paul's circumstances.

Because the country was at war sailors were often press-ganged into the Royal Navy to fight sea battles for the king. John was himself press-ganged as a teenager. Many countries have compulsory national service. Do you think everyone should serve their country in the armed forces for a year or two? Do you think Christians should be in the armed forces at all, or should they be pacifists? There are several Old Testament examples of God telling his people to fight for what was right.

Chapter Eight
All Change!

John was sure God wanted him to be a minister, but it was six years before the church ordained him. All that time John worked away in Liverpool. Are you patient when you have to wait for things? King David has something to say about patience. See Psalm 37:7. Paul says that patience is part of a chain of learning. Work out the links in the chain from Romans 5:4-5.

Although John Newton had no children of his own he befriended children in Olney. Some of his young friends were very poor and real troublemakers. Do we think God is only interested in clean and well-dressed people? If a poor and dirty person came into your church would he be made to feel welcome? Jesus has some advice for us. See Luke 14:12-14.

John wasn't ashamed of being seen in the street with his young friends. Are you sometimes embarrassed to be seen with someone whose street cred is low?

Chapter Nine

The Collapse of a Camel

Betsy's grandfather thought middle-aged parents and life in a minister's home would be very dull for a little girl. Should Christians be dull people? Is there anything wrong with believers laughing and enjoying themselves? The New Testament says a lot about joy. See Philippians 4:4. But are there some things that Christians should not allow themselves to enjoy: some jokes, programmes and books?

John's Newton wrote many hymns. The most famous of them is Amazing Grace. John found it amazing that God in his grace should have saved him from his sins. Is it only amazing when God saves terrible sinners like slave-ship captains? Is it any less amazing when God saves 'good' people? Is there anyone who, in God's eyes, is so good that he doesn't need to be saved? See Romans 3:10-12. What happens to the Christian's sins after he is forgiven? Romans 4:7-8 gives you a clue.

Chapter Ten

Satan, Self and Company

In John Newton's day a fifth of all children died before they grew up. Today, in the Western world, very few children die. Have you known a child who died? Are you able to trust that God always does right, even when someone dies young? See Genesis 18:25.

John had some interesting visitors to his vestry. Was he right to be concerned about the woman who won the lottery? Do you think the lottery is just good fun or is it gambling? Is it wrong to gamble? What about the good causes that benefit from the lottery? Do you think Christians would be better to give their money directly to the good causes?

The wealthy men who complained about the stock-market didn't get much sympathy from John Newton. What does the Bible say about loving money? See Matthew 6:24. Does Matthew 6:19 mean that we shouldn't save money, or that it should not be what we love most?

Chapter Eleven

Enter William Wilberforce

When William came to see John Newton he didn't want his friends to know about it. Are you sometimes embarrassed by your faith? Do you try to be a secret Christian? Jesus understood that temptation and warned against it. See Matthew 5:14-16. According to what Jesus says, what won't happen if you are a secret Christian?

It took courage for William to fight the slave trade because some very important people were making money from it. Do you ever chicken out of doing things so as not to offend important people? Would you play in a school sports fixture rather than admit to your coach that you'd rather go to church? See Deuteronomy 31:6. It takes courage to do what is right. Think of the areas of your life that are difficult. Could it be because you're not aware that God is with you? Remember he is right beside you when the going gets tough.

Chapter Twelve
Victory at Long Last!

John could not undo what he had done to the slaves he bought in West Africa and sold to plantation owners. But he did what he could to help set them free. Can you undo what you've done in the past, or un-say words that you're sorry you said? Are there some people to whom you need to apologise? Is there anything you can do for friends or family members you've hurt in the past?

Mary and John Newton loved each other very much. Over the years they were married he prayed that she would never become an idol to him, that he would never love her too much. What does God say about idolatry? See Exodus 20:4-5. But the Bible also says that husbands and wives have to love each other very, very much. Ephesians 5:22-33 paints a picture of a good marriage. Have you ever thought of praying for the person God may want you to marry? You could pray that God will keep him / her special for you, and keep you special for him or her.

Prayer Diary

Prayer is another word for communicating with God. We can talk to him about our concerns and problems. We can talk to him to tell him our feelings. We can talk to him to tell him how much we love him and to thank him for all the wonderful things he has done for us. It is also important to talk to God about our mistakes and the wrong things we have done. This is called confession. If you want a little guide to show you how to pray use the following word:

A C T S

A   **stands for Adoration.**
This means love.
Tell God how you love him.

C   **stands for Confession.**
This means telling God about
what you have done wrong.
Tell God that you are sorry
for the wrong things you have
done.

T   **stands for Thanks.**
Thank God for what he gives
you every day, for his Word the
Bible and for his free offer of
salvation.

S   **stands for Supplication.**
This means asking for things.
Ask God for what you need.
Ask him for help and comfort and
for all the things you need day by
day. Ask him for the forgiveness
of your sins and for help to obey
him and follow him.

Prayer Diary for a Week

Sunday

Although John Newton believed that his father loved him, he didn't feel loved.

Pray for parents who can't show affection.

Pray for children whose parents have never told them they love them.

Ask God's blessing on children whose parents have abused them. Pray that such children will be given all the help and support they need to stop them becoming abusers too.

Remember your parents in prayer. Being a teenager is hard work, and being a parent is just as hard. Ask God to help you understand your parents, and to help them to understand you.

Pray that when you grow up you might be loving and caring to those closest to you.

Monday

John Newton's mother died when he was a very little boy. His father married again. He had a little half-brother by his father's second marriage.

Pray for children and young people who have lost a parent, whether by death, divorce or separation. Ask God to help you understand those of your friends who no longer live with both their parents.

Remember stepmothers and stepfathers, praying that

they might learn to love their stepchildren. And ask the Lord to be especially close to those who feel pushed out when a new baby is born into the family.

If you are a stepchild, pray that you will be able to love and respect your stepparent.

Tuesday

As a teenager, John Newton had some narrow escapes. They made him think about what would happen if he died, but they didn't leave any lasting effect.

Ask God to keep you safe from illness and injury. Pray for those you know who are unwell or who have been hurt in any way.

When things happen that make you really think about the Lord, pray that you won't push them to the back of your mind as John Newton did. Let God speak to you through want happens to you and around you.

Pray for any you know who are ill or have been hurt in accidents, and for the families of any who have died.

Wednesday

John Newton was working full-time by his eleventh birthday.

In many parts of the world children don't really have a childhood; they are working as soon as they are old enough. Pray for these children, especially those in countries like India who work in factories that produce some of the designer goods you wear. Many of them work in places where little attention is paid to their health and safety.

Pray for young people in this country who go out to work to earn some extra money. Ask God to help you not to join the rat race of always wanting more and more things and to remind you of those who have little or nothing at all.

Thursday

John Newton lived long enough to see the slave trade abolished in Britain. But slavery is still a problem today.

Those who suffer from addictions are slaves to what addicts them. Pray for those among your friends who have addiction problems: those who smoke, over-eat or starve themselves; for those who drink, take drugs or can't stop themselves lying and cheating.

Ask God to protect you from temptation to do things that might lead to addiction. And if you do have a problem already, pray that he will give you strength to get through it by taking just one day at a time.

Pray for those in some parts of the world who are still in slavery, just as people were in John Newton's day.

Friday

John Newton left the slave trade because he had a seizure. That was confusing for him at the time, though he was very grateful for it eventually.

Pray for those of your friends who have health problems and whose career choices seem limited by them. It may be that you are in this situation. Ask God to help you and them to understand that he uses such circumstances in people's lives to lead them to where he wants them to be.

Life doesn't always go according to our hopes and plans. Pray that when things don't seem to be working out the way you want them, that you'll be able to look at your circumstances and see what God wants you to do.

Saturday

John Newton was able to move on. From being a slave ship captain he became a campaigner against the slave trade.

Pray that you might have the courage to change your mind, and to admit that you were wrong.

Ask God to bless people in authority: parents, teachers, elected rulers etc., praying especially that they might be given open minds and the courage to change their views on things.

Pray for those who are brave enough to stand up for what they believe is right and to fight against evil things in our society. Pray for any social campaigners you know, either personally or from the television or newspapers. Ask God to show you if there is anything you should be prepared to campaign about.

Answers

Some of the Thinking Further topics require specific answers. The following will help answer some of these. Not all the answers are included as many of the questions are given purely as discussion starters.

Chapter 2
Jesus wept at the graveside of his friend Lazarus. We should feel sad when people die and even when Christians die. There is nothing wrong with this, but when Christians die we know that they have gone to be with the Lord Jesus Christ. We should not be sorrowful like those who have no hope of eternal life.

Chapter 3
Parents generally know what is best for us and we should ask advice from parents and from others who are more experienced and wiser than us.

Chapter 4
There is a difference between living a good life and being a Christian. Living a good life will not get us into heaven but trusting in the Lord Jesus Christ for the forgiveness of our sins through his death for us on the cross will give us eternal life when we die. We will be in heaven with the Lord Jesus Christ. A Christian is someone who trusts Jesus.

Chapter 5
Christians can have a good influence on their society and communities. Christians can influence people and

communities in their world ... to lead them away from sin which is like a spiritual decay. Christians can be used to bring God's Word and power into the world and to change lives.

Chapter 6
Solomon said, 'He who loves his son is careful to discipline him.' Discipline is an important part of child rearing.

Chapter 9
All have sinned and fallen short of the glory of God. So all of us need to be saved - no exceptions. Jesus is the only one who lived a perfect life. Once you are forgiven God will cover over your sins and not think about them any more. You are no longer guilty - Christ has taken your guilt upon himself.

Chapter 12
Idolatry is forbidden in God's Word. It is not permitted to worship anything or anyone else other than the one true God.

Trailblazers Series

HISTORY LIVES SERIES

Peril and Peace,
Chronicles of the Ancient Church
History Lives, Volume 1
ISBN: 978-184550-082-5

Read the stories of Paul, Polycarp, Justin, Origen, Cyprian, Constantine, Athanasius, Ambrose, Augustine, John Chrysostom, Jerome, Patrick, and Benedict.

Monks and Mystics,
Chronicles of the Medieval Church
History Lives, Volume 2
ISBN: 978-1-84550-083-2

Read the stories of Gregory the Great, Boniface, Charlemagne, Constantine Methodius, Vladimir, Anselm of Canterbury, Bernard of Clairvaux, Francis of Assisi, Thomas Aquinas, Catherine of Sienna, John Wyclif and John Hus.

Courage and Conviction,
Chronicles of the Reformation Church
History Lives, Volume 3
ISBN: 978-1-84550-222-5

Read the stories of the reformers in the 16th and 17th centuries who changed the face of the Christian church forever.

Hearts and Hands,
Chronicles of the Awakening Church
History Lives, Volume 4
ISBN: 978-1-84550-288-1

Read the stories of the gifted preachers and justice fighters who led the 1st & 2nd Great Awakenings in the 18th and 19th centuries.

The Adventures Series
An ideal series to collect

Amazon Adventures by Horace Banner
ISBN 978-1-85792-440-4

African Adventures by Dick Anderson
ISBN 978-1-85792-807-5

Great Barrier Reef Adventures by Jim Cromarty
ISBN 978-1-84550-068-9

Himalayan Adventures by Penny Reeve
ISBN 978-1-84550-080-1

Kiwi Adventures by Bartha Hill
ISBN 978-1-84550-282-9

Outback Adventures by Jim Cromarty
ISBN 978-1-85792-974-4

Rainforest Adventures by Horace Banner
ISBN 978-1-85792-627-9

Rocky Mountain Adventures by Betty Swinford
ISBN 978-1-85792-962-1

Scottish Highland Adventures by Catherine Mackenzie
ISBN 978-1-84550-281-2

Wild West Adventures by Donna Vann
ISBN 978-1-84550-065-8

CHRISTIAN FOCUS PUBLICATIONS

Christian Christian CF4K Mentor
Focus Heritage

Christian Focus Publications publishes books for adults and children under its four main imprints: Christian Focus, CF4K, Mentor and Christian Heritage. Our books reflect that God's word is reliable and Jesus is the way to know him, and live for ever with him.

Our children's publication list includes a Sunday school curriculum that covers pre-school to early teens; puzzle and activity books. We also publish personal and family devotional titles, biographies and inspirational stories that children will love.

If you are looking for quality Bible teaching for children then we have an excellent range of Bible story and age specific theological books.

From pre-school to teenage fiction, we have it covered!

**Find us at our web page:
www.christianfocus.com**

CF4·K
*Because you're never
too young to know Jesus*